T0327321

GREEN WOOD CARVING

GREEN WOOD CARVING

HOW TO MAKE BEAUTIFUL OBJECTS FROM UNSEASONED WOOD

HARALD LAMON

CONTENTS

TREES
- Joyce Kilmer

I think that I shall never see
A poem lovely as a tree.

A tree whose hungry mouth is prest
Against the earth's sweet flowing breast;

A tree that looks at God all day,
And lifts her leafy arms to pray;

A tree that may in Summer wear
A nest of robins in her hair;

Upon whose bosom snow has lain;
Who intimately lives with rain.

Poems are made by fools like me,
But only God can make a tree.

Heart
For Wood

FOREWORD BY LEE STOFFER

My fascination with what could be achieved with fresh-cut timber and simple hand tools was first sparked by watching Ray Mears' bushcraft shows on TV many years ago. A short while later I was further inspired and mentored by Mike Abbott, a highly respected and well-established green wood craftsman here in England, which at the time was quite a rare thing to be. Having embarked on my green wood journey as a hobby, it soon evolved into a big part of how I engaged with the world around me and eventually became a career, providing me an abundance of opportunities to connect with like-minded folk, share skills and spend many happy, productive times in woodlands around campfires, carving, cooking, chatting and creating fond memories.

More recently, I returned to the place where it all started for me – a beautiful woodland where Mike used to teach. Other friends I'd made along the way had continued to develop the place and were building a fantastic log cabin there. I had the privilege of getting involved with that project and, one day, while I was working away building a bespoke kitchen in the cabin, who should wander in but Mike, accompanied by his student for the week. He was a bold and colourful character from Belgium, who was learning chair-making skills and fancied a look around the woods. As I was introduced to Harald, he recognized me from a video on my friend Zed's YouTube channel and we quickly realized we'd have plenty to talk about. Soon after that we met again at yet another friend's spoon carving event, where we were both teaching but found time to get to know each other. Harald's warm-hearted enthusiasm and thirst for creative knowledge are apparent and infectious. Having since welcomed Harald into my life as a houseguest, curious and capable student, teacher and good friend, it was an honour that he asked me to be involved in helping to bring this fabulous book to an English-speaking audience.

I no longer think in terms of coincidence; for me, serendipity much better describes the seemingly unconnected but complementary events that make life sweeter when you take the time to notice them. As I was reviewing the translation of the chapters you are about to enjoy, my bedtime reading was Dick Proenneke's account of his time building his cabin (with hand tools) in the Alaskan wilderness, written over 50 years ago. I couldn't help but notice the similarities in the passion, commitment and connection with nature, complemented by the gratitude for a simpler life that both books conveyed. In essence, we are still beings who yearn for that natural connection despite all of our modern-day distractions. It's refreshing to read a contemporary book that harks back to simpler, as Harald might say, 'cosy' times. He has presented a wealth of knowledge, beautifully illustrated with practical advice and heartwarming observations in this engaging read that clearly shows he has a 'heart for wood'!

01

ONCE UPON A TIME...

People, trees and wood

WORKING GREEN, FRESH WOOD WITH HAND TOOLS IS PERHAPS AS OLD AS MANKIND ITSELF. **Fresh wood is softer to process using hand tools and easier to split**. Unlike sawn wood, each piece of split wood retains its strength and uniqueness. While practising my craft, one of the most beautiful moments is when I cleave a fresh piece of wood in half with my axe. It feels like unwrapping a special gift without yet knowing what is inside. In such a moment, I feel connected **to nature and the tree that once was**.

Every type of wood works, smells and feels different. The trees that produce the wood are always unique and usually originate in the place I feel at home: the forest. Trees have their own history. Their annual rings and growth sometimes tell us more about the history and climate of our past, which is studied in chronodendrology. Trees can grow to be much older than us, up to even thousands of years old, and they have been around much longer than humans. Trees are a crucial part of nature and forest ecosystems. Trees are commonplace and mysterious at the same time and sometimes seem to be part of our world in a very different way, and at a different pace.

I love trees and used to want to climb them all the time. I may not hug them, but I can often get quite near to a giant in the forest that gives life to so many animals and fungi or be amazed by an acorn that has such a small chance of becoming a giant oak (less than 0.00001%, apparently) but still tries to grow. The more I discover and learn, the more I realize how special they really are and how little people know about trees; how they grow and live, how they communicate with each other and how they are connected to the life surrounding them.

Worldwide, 17,500 tree species are in danger of extinction; that is almost 30 per cent of nearly 60,000 known species. It is estimated that 10,000 species are still to be discovered in our jungles. That means there are twice as many endangered tree species on our planet as endangered animal species. The biggest threats to trees are cutting them down to make way for agriculture and cattle ranching, timber exports and climate change and its accompanying temperature rise. I am familiar with the wood from our forests and gardens here in Belgium. That's barely 100 species. **Trees and shrubs constitute an incredible wealth of species**, of which few people are aware. Some even consider them merely as decoration for our planet. Every day I learn. As often is the case with people, we have to get to know something before we learn to love it and find the strength to want to protect it.

The piece of wood connects me to nature around me, but the axe or knife in my hand brings a secondary **connection as a human being: to billions of people before me**.

Human history is inextricably linked to the use of cutting tools. From sharp flint shards to a fist axe to which a handle was later attached – the first hatchet. Later, axes and knives were made from copper and bronze, then from iron and eventually from the most modern and strongest steels. Knives and axes shaped our history over a period of more than two million years, enabled progress and accelerated our evolution.

Wood carving – or more broadly, working fresh wood with hand tools – has a long but also very diverse history. In my daily work, I feel inspired by, broadly, four different influences and wood workers from our past:

Many techniques and tools I use every day have their origins in **ancient crafts**. Some are very technical, such as chair making, and require years of practice and refinement to become a master of the craft. At the height of the craft period, just before the Industrial Revolution, the manual working of (fresh) wood was increasingly divided into different specializations and professions. With heavy axes and giant saws, lumberjacks went into the forest every day to fell ancient trees, after which sawyers sawed out planks and other parts. Wood turners used to go to the forest themselves to turn chair legs and spindles on the spot. Spoon carvers needed less wood, but ship and mast builders needed more. Everything made of wood had its specialist – a **master craftsman** doing only one part of the work in the process from tree to finished product.

Secondly, what I do can also be traced back to every human being who once made something out of a branch with a pocketknife. In English, this is called **whittling;** in Dutch, unfortunately, we don't have an inspiring translation for it. So, it's 'wood carving' – not as a profession or necessity – but as a **creative and relaxing activity**. This makes me think of a cowboy whittling a small horse by the campfire, a shepherd in the mountains whittling patterns into his walking stick or an old father somewhere in a cabin in the dark north spending his evenings by the stove whittling. This form of carving is much more approachable and belongs to all times and cultures. As a boy, I remember the special power that emanated from a frugal pocketknife and the myriad possibilities of what it could do with a branch. In the end, it often became just a sharp point that then represented a spear in our war game, or an arrow fired from a crossbow of bendable curtain rods. I still find that special feeling every day in the things I make.

The third influence in my daily work is the many **wood artists** over the centuries who made sculptures, musical instruments, special pieces of furniture or decorative carvings out of wood. Unfortunately, I neither have such talent nor the patience it requires. Thanks to all these creative minds, who bring out the inherent and **special beauty of wood,** wood still has a place in our arts and in our homes.

My last and perhaps greatest inspiration originates from the **First Nations of North America**. Especially as a spoon carver, I am truly amazed by some tribes making everything with just four tools. From their wigwams and bows to canoes, snowshoes and dream catchers. The only tools they had – or needed – were an axe, a knife, a mocotaugan and an awl.

A mocotaugan is a crooked knife with a handle tailored to the user. It is both a spoon knife, which I use daily for hollowing out, and a one-handed drawknife to work long branches for paddles, for example. I made my own mocotaugan out of oak, with a handle that fits my hand perfectly. At the bottom of the tang, the metal is bent to fit into a slot in the handle. Together with the binding, this ensures that the blade remains fixed in the handle without glue.

Making it was enough of a challenge, but only when you learn how to use it can you understand the craftsmanship of people who carried all their tools on their belts. Clamping was done with their bodies – they didn't need a workbench. Wood working was not a craft or profession, but an **essential part of their daily life**, producing for themselves what they needed from the raw materials provided by forests and animals.

Thanks to the efforts of all these wood workers and artists, tools for turning trees into wood and wood into objects, houses and sculptures have also continued to evolve. Fortunately, there are still blacksmiths today who make solid wood carving tools. For every task, the appropriate knife, gouge, drill, chisel, axe, adze or saw is available somewhere. Regularly, new tools are still invented and improved to cater for the ever-growing group of wood workers. Really exciting!

It seems contradictory, loving trees and wood carving, but it has never been like that for me. It always feels like a special way of **using your mind and your hands to work a material that has always been part of human culture, right from our earliest beginnings.**

I have always worked respectfully **with wood** and feel a growing responsibility to carry that part of my work outward. I will never cut a tree, branch or bush just for the sake of carving. In our forest, cutting any piece of wood is done in accordance with forest management. However, most of the wood I get comes from friends and many others who support my work and like the fact that wood from their gardens gets a second life. I try to make use of every piece of a branch or log and to manage our piece of forest with knowledge and skill so that it benefits the forest and its inhabitants.

Using local wood and hand tools is a **sustainable way of creating things** that makes me proud. Creating things yourself from a tree makes you think about how other objects are made and especially what impact this has on our planet. This is not self-evident in stuff that is available in shops and for sale. Stuff is made somewhere and transported; it requires raw materials and machinery and personnel. In that often very long chain in time and distance, many choices can be made. This also raises the question of what we buy and why we buy it. What value do we attach to things and the way they are made? Do we need them at all, or who says we need them? What value do they add to our lives and how do we want to live?

The difference between handmade wooden items and mass-produced ones is enormous, in so many ways, and is symbolic of how we could make different choices or **treat trees and nature differently**. I am not a green saint, nor do I know who made my shoes or where some of that delicious food I eat every day comes from. Nor do I know where every part of this laptop comes from. I do try, increasingly, and I hope to inspire others to try too. **Maybe the wood in our lives is a great place to start**.

I realize that what I do is a luxury. Not all of us have the luxury of having time off to carve wood or take a workshop with me to learn how to do it. People who buy something from me have money enough to cook with handmade wooden spoons or have wooden coat hooks to hang their jackets on. My job and my passion can only exist because of that luxury. Though, maybe it is not a luxury, but a basic right to have the time and space to do what you love. A hundred years ago, the spoon carver in Flanders was a poor craftsman and the wooden spoons he made were for the even poorer peasant. Whichever way you look at it, I believe it is precisely this kind of luxury in our lives that gives us the opportunity and space to make different choices and to live and consume differently. **The handmade wooden spoon: perhaps a symbol of change**.

A HEART FOR WOOD

My love for wood and wood carving has always been there, but **the path to it was not obvious**. As a child, I remember many hours spent tinkering with a pocketknife, saw, hammer and nails to make bows, swords, shields and everything else that was part of my imagination at the time. Later, I started making furniture for my own bedroom. In my adolescence, playing with wood was less normal for my peers and at school it was more important to study hard than be creative. At that time, there was an old stone sharpening wheel in the shed next to the house where we lived. I had no clue about grinding then, but if you pushed wooden sticks against such a wheel, the wood would start to burn and you could make unusual patterns with those black lines. I secretly felt like an inventor and that was great.

Once at university, while studying psychology, I again felt the urge to work with wood. I enrolled in a traditional wood carving course. By traditional, I mean wood carving with chisels and gouges in perfectly dried and straight oak planks to make carvings, like the ones you see on confessionals in church. This course was not quite what I was looking for to get creative with wood. Chisels and wood were expensive for a student and a workbench wouldn't fit in my student room. But I did learn a lot about wood and tools then. Only later did I realize the value of these classes.

Later, when I settled down, wood was mainly a material for remodelling and renovation. I learnt to work with machines. Then we moved to a house with a big garden and I tried again to build with branches and be creative with wood. Together with my sons, I finally rediscovered the child in myself and made a two-storey tree house and a 538 sq ft (50 sq m) oak shed in the garden.

Writing all of this, it seems obvious that I would be absolutely thrilled when I saw someone making a spoon out of a branch about 12 years ago, using only an axe, a knife and a spoon knife. I finally felt like I knew what to do with wood. It seemed completely right; **it almost felt like coming home.** I wondered why I hadn't thought of it myself for the previous 30 years. It started with the first spoon I carved then – and part of the journey I've taken since then can be found in this book (called *Heart for Wood* in the original Dutch edition).

LEARNING FROM MASTERS

After that first spoon, progress was slow. Ten years ago, there were not many books or videos about green wood working or spoon carving. I also had little time for it, or rather I made too little time for it, with a busy job, renovations, young children and free time that was then mostly filled with bushcraft. For years, spoon carving was something for a free Sunday afternoon or an unexpected energy boost after a long working day. **In the beginning, I often felt frustrated.** I felt it didn't go the way it should: it took a long time and I began to realize more and more that I lacked a lot of knowledge and basic skills. The available courses were limited and not always that good, but with each course my ability and knowledge advanced. I invested in myself and what I loved doing, pursuing a pleasure I knew would one day come.

My spoons got better, prettier and more useful, and began to get nice reactions from those around me. Here and there I even got a request to give a workshop. I had already given several bushcraft workshops and for this target group a carving workshop was a nice addition and easy to integrate. **A difficult start gave way to pride, satisfaction and flow while making.** I began to feel that I wanted to do this for the rest of my life. Hard work and lots of practice eventually resulted in something good. This is in contrast to pursuits that provide quick gratification and with very little value to yourself and your own evolution. Practice makes craft. But the most important lesson for me was that good education makes this process so much faster and more achievable. **It was my responsibility to seek that education and make time for it**. I read every new book that came out, in different languages, went abroad to take courses in many more subjects than spoon carving and devoured the ever-growing supply of YouTube videos.

In 2019, I received my first **scholarship as a master in a master-apprentice programme** awarded by the Flemish government, in Belgium. A great reward for hard work and confidence in my dreams and plans. This programme and the resulting funding were a tipping point and brought me a step closer to taking the big leap. I gave up my job as coordinator of a youth residential centre and started **the Spoonhouse** (www.lepelhuis.be).

I give courses and workshops to young and old in various disciplines of green wood working. The Spoonhouse in Bruges, Belgium is our home, my workshop and shop where I sell everything I make. There is a sign on the window: 'I'm open when I'm at home'. So, everyone is always welcome when I'm home, from early morning to late at night! Just ring the bell if you're in the area or make an appointment if you want to be sure. My life is filled with interesting projects, workshops, creative studio days, Spoon Club, Spoonfests, beautiful encounters and promising plans. Besides the Spoonhouse, we also have **the Spoonforest**, our little piece of paradise here on Earth. This piece of woodland in Torhout, Belgium is where most of the workshops take place and where I really feel at home under the big oaks in the outdoor workplace.

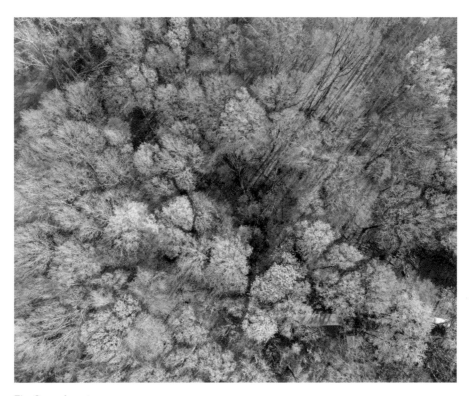

The Spoonforest

For my students, I try to be the teacher I would have liked to find myself in those first years in our small country. I wrote this book with the same question in the back of my mind: what would I have wanted to read ten years ago?

Although it never feels like work, being a craftsman is something that never stops, starts or ends. It is a way of life. When I take a bike ride with my wife, she sees all the shops, beautiful houses and cosy streets along the way. I, however, mostly see all the trees and bushes, all the wooden structures, studios and creative, unique constructions. We always see the world from our own perspective. **Trees are the common thread in my life** and my future is as exciting and multifaceted as the wood I work with every day. It's not always sunshine and roses, but I am a happy person.

WHAT IS CRAFT OR HANDMADE?

Craft is about choices made at every step of the process, about **how the mind, hands, heart and wood work together**. With a craft, there is not only value in the final product, but also in the process itself. It's about how the maker adds something personal to the product; how the imperfect beauty of the wood ensures that each piece is unique. It is about **balancing the functionality of the product, the creativity and identity of the maker, and the properties and limits of the wood the maker is working with**. The most important question may not even be how something is made, but whether there is a meaning in the story of the maker that moves or inspires you. It is about the pride of making something good and the pleasure of using something unique that will last a very long time. Wood carving is good for us, and I will come back to that later!

To me, handmade certainly does not mean that machines can't be used. Just like a knife or an axe, a machine can become an extension of our own bodies and a means of transferring our ideas into the wood. Machinery can also benefit the creative process by speeding up certain steps, freeing up more time for something else. Again, balance is of the essence. I have a few machines that I use on a regular basis, some of which will also be covered in this book. The chainsaw, for example – my dangerous friend that allows me to divide large pieces of a tree very quickly into promising pieces of wood that will later become spoons, bowls or kuksas for me or my students. I also have a good drill that makes drilling large holes so much easier. You also need to strike a balance when using your own muscle power and physical labour. Machinery can save energy that you can use much better elsewhere. I hope all the steps in this book show that craft is therefore about making choices. My choices can help you move forward, but **keep feeling the freedom to go your own way.** Craft is not a tightly defined process. It is precisely this freedom that makes our work special, as an expression of ourselves.

A BOOK IS NEVER FINISHED

My wife often describes me as sloppy and a perfectionist at the same time. By now, Jonathan, my publisher at GMC, also knows what that means. All these words, ideas and feelings have been in my head for a long time. It has been quite a job to get them on paper in a readable, inspiring and structured way and then translate them into English. My head sometimes feels like my workshop: chaotic, creative and full of possibilities, but with an underlying order and structure that, unfortunately, is not always immediately obvious to others at first glance.

Writing a book does something to a person. It has made me take a much closer look at and analyse my own way of working and making. I have also been forced to put dormant feelings and ideas into words and bring them into focus, for myself and for anyone reading this book. The step-by-step instructions have put my teaching under a magnifying glass. Now, I think I better understand what someone needs to learn to take the next step in their creative process. Creating a book requires a certain amount of vulnerability and opening yourself up to reaction and criticism. It also creates expectations that I hope will be met. In any case, I am happy with the process I went through. **It has enriched my life and my craft**, improved my time management and

brought new, beautiful people into my life. For me, a book is never finished and certainly not perfect. I see it more as **a record of the extraordinary journey** I have taken so far, from my first wooden spoon to the chance I was given and took to never have to work again. As you read this, book two on spoons and book three on stools are already starting to form in my head.

But first, this book. *Green Wood Carving* is best read from front to back the first time. Some chapters rely on the knowledge I've covered in earlier chapters or on tools I've described earlier. I have tried to find a good balance between tools that are really necessary and nice-to-haves; there are different paths that lead to virtuous wood carving and that suit your situation. If you have any comments or questions, or just want to let me know what you think of the book, please let me know – sincerely please – at harald@lepelhuis.be!

This is not an inspirational book, or rather, that is not my main intention. Thanks to social media, the beautiful work of very talented green wood carvers from all over the world is easy to look at for inspiration. Many books on wood carving are also particularly inspiring, but I have focused on elaborating on things more technically or explaining them in depth. Blended with stories, this makes the book a beautiful whole.

My first and foremost ambition is to make you eager to carve! Eager to make something beautiful or useful out of wood with axe and knife. **Eager to** create, share and experience it with others. **Eager to** express yourself creatively and feel connected to nature and human history. But above all, this is meant as a basic guide providing solid, complete and easy-to-understand explanations of how to create something beautiful and/or useful and how to carve safely. Mastering the basics ensures pleasure in carving and makes it feasible to shape your own creative ideas from a block of fresh wood. I experience this pleasure and satisfaction every day by teaching and guiding others. That is why this book is both a reference and at the same time **a thank you to all the course participants of the past years**. It is not an easy-to-read bedside table book. Certainly, the practical chapters need to be waded through rather than read lying down. During my workshops, I always try to explain the sometimes technical side of wood carving as well as possible and to make it understandable. This book is the continuation of that.

I hope you get even more inspired, but above all I hope you will feel **eager,** learn, be surprised and amazed about wood and wood carving and join me **in spreading this beautiful craft, passion or hobby**. Text and pictures may never be able to completely replace the interaction, atmosphere and explanations on site and certainly not the warm cosy glow of the campfire, but I really tried my best. **Welcome to the beautiful world of green wood working**.

HARALD

WORDS OF GRATITUDE

Thanks to

Jonathan at GMC, for your trust in me and your belief that what I do can inspire others. But also for your critical thoughts based on years of experience, knowledge about books and people.

Véronique, photographer, for your incredible talent to translate my reality into beautiful images that allow others to really feel and understand what I want to describe.

Nico, for the drawings that clarify what photos cannot, one of your many talents.

Tom Joye of Natuurinvest, because your knowledge of trees goes beyond my books.

All students, participants, customers, fellow wood carvers and friends of the Spoon Club. Your enthusiastic eagerness to learn, your support and gratitude motivate me every day to continue on this journey and you challenge me to do better and better. You bring out the best in me. Thank you for all those beautiful moments in the forest or workshop. In particular, I would like to thank Andy and Thomas for your patience and trust, Ruben for the beautiful drone photos of the Spoonforest and Rinus for all the help and beautiful moments in the forest!

My teachers over the years, including **Fritiof Runhall, Mikey Elefant, Mike Abbott, Sean Hellman and Ben Willis**. You are an inspiration to me and many others. True craftsmen in a special contemporary sense of the word. In particular, I would also like to thank **Sjors at VersHout and Lee Stoffer**, both dear friends, colleagues, sounding boards, examples in craft and life and beautiful human beings!

My old friends, for your friendship and continued belief in the choices I make and the dreams we share, especially Steven and Wendy for your help and enthusiasm.

My critical readers Jan, Jonas, Pernel and Dries. You have risen to the great challenge of transforming my storytelling narrative into a strong and clear text that expresses even more beautifully what I wanted to say. Dries, you were essential to make my Dutch come to life in English!

My sister, for your enthusiasm, special support and much help in the forest and in taking the hundreds of step-by-step photos for this book. You are the invisible hand behind this book, but present on almost every page.

My parents and family, for your proud care and unconditional support in my special journey through life. My father-in-law Chris, an extra thank you for the beautiful close-ups.

Our children, for your amazement, sneaky pride and love!

My wife, the rock and foundation on which my Spoonhouse is built, my most critical reader and my walking stick on this particular and challenging path we choose every day.

02

WOOD IN A NUTSHELL

As old as mankind

WOOD FLOWS LIKE BLOOD THROUGH THE VEINS OF HUMAN HISTORY AND OUR DAILY LIVES. From our cradle to our coffin, throughout our lives, wood is so naturally present that we rarely stop to think about it. From early copper and iron smelting, wheels, windmills, Viking ships and wine barrels to spoons and Stradivarius violins. Wood brings warmth and provides shelter. Its smoke can help preserve our food. Tannins in wood were indispensable in making leather. Gums and resins as well as various dyes and fragrances are derived from wood. And of course, the book you hold in your hands, like millions of books printed before it, has wood as its origin. Superior skills with wood played an inordinate role in our evolution. **Try to imagine what human history would have been like without trees providing us with wood or the skills to harness it.**

Wood is a material that survives the test of time. As a result, it is not surprising that it is not just objects that were kept in tombs that have survived from ancient times. At the Louvre in Paris, many wooden objects such as jewellery, boxes, bowls and chairs from various Egyptian dynasties can be admired. These are real works of art with very fine carvings. They were important enough – alongside other objects in gold or silver – to be buried with the pharaoh.

In Ireland, wooden spoons with traces of butter over 3,000 years old have been found. The Greeks and Romans also had wooden spoons, bowls, dishes and furniture. And in Belgium, 'old' wood can still be seen in the beautiful roof trusses of the Ter Doest Abbey barn, whose timber was cut between 1365 and 1370.

There was a special discovery in Sweden – the approximately 1,000-year-old Mästermyr toolbox containing, among other things, a carving knife, adze, drawknives and axes. Exactly the tools we still use today. Sweden is also one of the few countries where the craft of wood working in fresh wood is still taught in colleges today. Even in primary education, the 'slöjd method' (manual skills and craftsmanship) is included in the curriculum of a lot of schools.

This book focuses on relatively simple hand-carved and unique objects that almost everyone takes for granted, such as spoons in the kitchen. In the past, these were mostly carved from fresh wood. A little digging into my local Flemish history here in Belgium reveals how these objects were also part of our culture and daily use. One of the finest examples can be found in the paintings of Pieter Bruegel the Elder. In the painting *The Peasant Wedding* from 1567, for example, you can see how the guests' benches and stools are made of legs of round wood, attached with mortise-and-tenon joints to planks. The legs often still show traces of bark, indicating green wood working. The guests at the table eat with wooden spoons and the carrier in the front has tucked his own wooden spoon into his hat. But the cutest thing is the little child in the front of the painting who has his pocketknife hanging from his belt, even at a wedding.

Other sources and examples can also be found in the image gallery of the Centre for Agricultural History. There you will find many pictures of (milk) stools and wooden fruit baskets made of cleaved slats from the 18th and 19th centuries. At the Roman Archaeological Museum (RAM) in Oudenburg, Belgium you can see many beautiful hand-carved objects from Roman times. At Erfgoedplus.be you can find a wealth of green wood tools and objects made throughout our history.

The industrialization of labour and internationalization of trade meant that the last chair makers, basket weavers, lath cutters, spoon carvers and other green wood craftsmen in Flanders retired at the beginning of the 20th century. **It is incredible to think that a few generations ago there were still Flemish people who earned their living with these crafts and how quickly the memory of them is lost.** What used to be in the minds, hands and also hearts of many could not be learnt anywhere for a long time. All that remained for many people was 'playing' with a stick and a pocketknife. Now, we are at a new beginning and this book intends to contribute to giving green wood working a new, meaningful, living and sustainable future.

Green wood carving, a craft

I USE WOOD THAT IS FRESH AND THEREFORE STILL CONTAINS A LOT OF SAP OR WATER. That makes it easier to carve because the water acts as a lubricant for the tools, so to speak. We could also produce everything in this book from dry wood, but it would require much more effort. Green wood carving refers to a process that is totally different from, on the one hand, the contemporary use of sheet materials, for example, in which wood is sometimes hard to find. And, on the other hand, it is also totally different from processing perfectly dried wood with lathes or computer-driven cutting machines.

The process is completely different, founded on the difference between craft and production. But the final product, in particular, reflects the huge difference that distinguishes green wood working from other forms of wood working.

It is the balance between three important elements that makes the product what it really is. It is about **the tree and the wood, about the function of the object and about the maker and his skills**. Balance means that none of the elements should dominate or the product will be reduced to just one element.

A beautifully hand-carved kuksa allows the wood to express its beauty and uniqueness; the function of such a wooden bowl is clear and practical; and the maker has left his mark through his design and the marks left by his tools. Straight, machine-made wooden spoons focus one-sidedly on function and neglect the creator's creative process in combination with the wood. Sleek designer tables made of first choice French oak reduce the wood to a small selection of its properties and break the link with the tree's natural growth with knots and gnarls. But the wood itself can also dominate one-sidedly. Smooth-sanded cutting boards or bowls from whimsical olive wood focus entirely on the splendour of this beautiful wood but sometimes neglect function, and the creative process is usually secondary to the price of production.

This special balance is how I evaluate and try to frame my work. Now and then something I make is out of balance or not quite what I had in mind and then this balance helps me. For you, dear reader, it might be different, but it can be interesting to look at wooden utensils in this way. Anyone who works with wood while appreciating its natural origins will never get a perfect result. Perfection is also not what I try to achieve. **To me, perfection in craft is diametrically opposed to freedom**. That does not mean that something cannot be beautifully finished, but by staying closer to the natural and rich variation of wood, each piece is unique. **There is beauty in imperfection,** especially when you embrace the unpredictability of wood. This means that I seldom use decoration or paint my spoons so as not to take attention away from the wood. On the other hand, with shrink pots, I feel I can use decoration, because the story of the wood is inherently linked to how such a pot is made.

Anatomy of wood

THE CROSS-SECTION OF THE TRUNK OF THIS OAK FROM THE SPOONFOREST SHOWS LIFE FROM THE BEGINNING AT THE HEART OF THE TREE TO ITS DEATH AT THE EDGE (see page 34). The annual rings witness a unique contrast between consistency and variation. You don't need to be a dendrologist to notice the beauty of wood or to be able to work with it. But **understanding what wood is, how it grows, moves and its special relationship to water makes your job as a green wood worker easier and more efficient.** It also brings more opportunities to get the most out of the wood and its characteristics.

At first, I did not feel the need for a deep dive into the study of wood. I feared perhaps this would take away the beauty and the magic. Nothing was further from the truth: **wood is fascinating and continues to amaze me**. The more you learn about something, the more you realize you know very little. It is no different with trees and wood. What follows is only an introduction to the life of a tree, but sufficient as a basis for the rest of this book.

When talking about wood we refer to shrubs and trees, which can be divided into deciduous trees (angiosperms) and conifers (dicotyledons). Other species that also make woody fibres, such as bamboo, wood ferns or palm trees, have a completely different structure and are outside the scope of this book. Woody growth can actually be seen as secondary growth after the first stage of primary or herbaceous growth of plants. Deciduous trees go one step further and form wood, so to speak, although every tree once started as a small herbaceous plant. Conifers have no herbaceous specimens and evolutionarily, the origin of wood is older than that of seed. Once there were wood-forming spore plants as ancestors, but unfortunately they perished. Apart from the seeds, resin, leaves and needles, there are also differences between coniferous and deciduous trees at the cellular level. I discuss this only where it is relevant to wood carving.

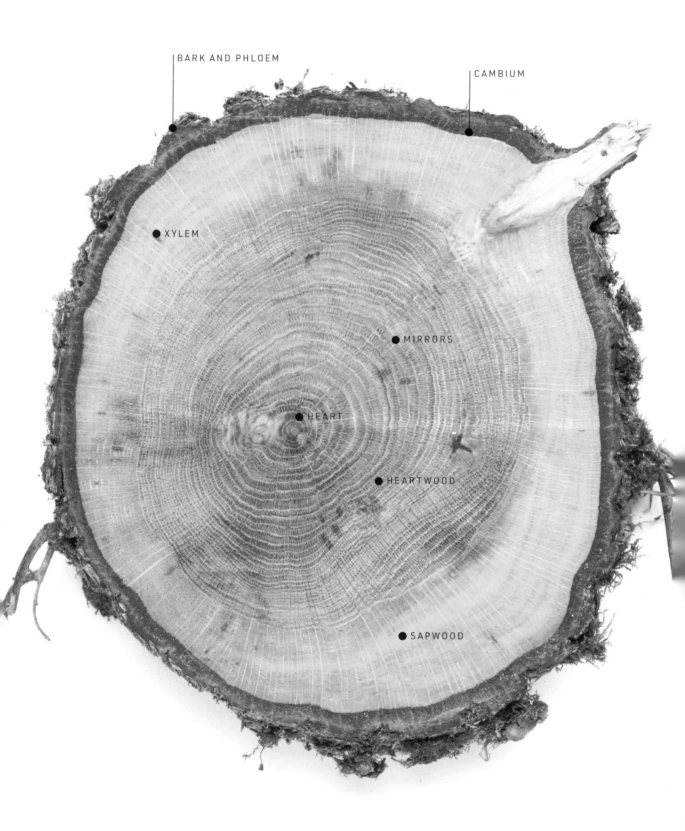

BARK AND PHLOEM

CAMBIUM

XYLEM

MIRRORS

HEART

HEARTWOOD

SAPWOOD

WHAT YOU SEE ON THE CROSS-SECTION:

1. Bark: outer bark and phloem The bark of a tree has two parts. The outer layer is the outer bark, which consists only of dead cells. They no longer provide transport but protect the tree. The bark is like the skin and the first defence against fungi, bacteria and insects. Under this outer bark is the second layer, the phloem, which is responsible for the downwards transportation of water and, especially, sugars, which are formed in the leaves as a result of photosynthesis – in addition to oxygen, of course. The distinction between bark and old sap channels of the phloem that are no longer operational is sometimes hard to see, making 'bark' a good umbrella term for all tissue outside the cambium layer.

2. The cambium is a thin layer of cells between the bark and the wood. It ensures the growth of a tree. The cambium forms new xylem cells on the inside and new phloem cells on the outside. In short, the cambium ensures the formation of wood and the growth of the tree.

3. The xylem is the actual wood of a tree and can consist of **heartwood** and **sapwood**. The sapwood is where the upward transportation of mainly water and dissolved minerals from the roots takes place. Heartwood is what we call 'dead wood'. It no longer provides transport; the cells are closed and, in some species, filled with core substances such as tannins, resins and oils, which can cause the dark colour. Heartwood is less moist than sapwood and mainly provides for the strength of the tree. Within the first annual rings you will find **the heart** of the wood, which is rarely, if ever, used.

On the cross-section you can also see shiny, radial lines, i.e. from the centre outwards (or vice versa). These are **the mirrors** or wood rays that provide for horizontal sap transport inside the tree. Sometimes they are also called pith rays, but since new ones are formed continually as the tree grows thicker, they do not all reach the heart or pith of the tree, which makes the name less applicable. Some, like oak, can have very nicely shaped wood rays; in other species they are not visible at all. Small rays can be seen as stripes in beech, maple and sycamore.

GROWTH OF TREES AND WOOD

The cambium is responsible for the tree's growth in both girth and height. Above and beside existing cells, new ones are formed. So, it is not that parts of trees grow longer or are stretched. If you were to drive a nail into a tree and cut that tree down 50 years later, you will find that the nail is still at the same height, but that it is now in the middle of the wood and has been overgrown by 50 years of growth. In other words, **the heart of a tree is that herbaceous tip from so many years ago that is still in the middle of the tree.** In elder, with its large pith inside, it is very clear to see that, like an onion, layers are constantly being added. The cambium circle slides along towards the outside, forming new wood inwards all the time.

Over the years branches become increasingly overgrown at their base by the trunk. The heart of a large branch always starts from the heart of the trunk. Branches that break off or rot close to the trunk are therefore also swallowed by the growth of the trunk outwards and, after years, become invisible on the outside. Before cleaving a trunk, I always try to predict what I will see.

Often it remains a surprise, but sometimes **subtle shapes or twists in the bark can tell you something about what's underneath.**

Trees and shrubs do not grow all year round here in Belgium, due to our seasonal climate. They are adapted to the seasons and grow only when there is sufficient water and light. In winter, trees do not grow in girth or height. Growth resumes in spring. **Earlywood or springwood** forms, which mainly provides sap flow in wide sap channels with thin cell walls. During summer, growth stalls due to heat. After the hottest part of summer, when more water is available again, the wood continues to grow in what we call **latewood or summerwood.** This layer mainly provides strength to the wood: it has thicker cell walls and is usually darker in colour than the pale earlywood. The annual rings are not clearly visible in all types of wood; much depends on the growing conditions. Annual rings help to determine the age of a tree, at least if you can see them on a disc that was cut close to the ground. The tropics have no seasons or, due to varying rainfall, several growth periods in a year, so there are no annual rings in wood there as we know them in trees from the climate here in Belgium.

Elder

Recognize and apply characteristics of wood species

WOOD HAS SPECIFIC PROPERTIES AND CHARACTERISTICS THAT CAN VARY GREATLY BETWEEN TREE SPECIES. However, different growing conditions can also make wood from the same tree species vary remarkably. On the one hand, these differences allow us to recognize species. On the other hand, these characteristics can be used to express the beauty or uniqueness of each wood species in the objects you make.

Recognizing wood is easiest if you can identify the tree. You can do this via the leaves or needles, buds, fruits and seeds, and it can also be done in combination with the silhouette or location of the tree. Recognizing trees is not easy at first. Good advice I once received myself was to start with a limited number of trees and not go out with a tree encyclopedia – in which case, you will soon fail to see the wood for the trees. I started off with five common species and tried to know and recognize all the properties of those trees in each season, as well as the properties of the wood in all its variations. Once you recognize those easily, you can add new ones to your collection. Little by little, you extend your knowledge and soon you will be able to identify most species in the forest.

I have my favourite sorts of wood but every part of the tree has its value and can be used. Below, I discuss their different characteristics and try, each time with examples, to help you learn and to recognize the different types of wood and hopefully appreciate and use the rich variety even more. Of course, a tree encyclopedia can tell you much more. I look at it from my perspective as a green wood worker.

HEARTWOOD
AND SAPWOOD

For outdoor applications of wood, this difference is extremely important, as heartwood is much more durable than sapwood. The sapwood cells are closed, the nutrients taken out and replaced by so-called extractive substances. Then it becomes heartwood. This ensures that heartwood is much less likely to be attacked by fungi or insects. For green wood processing, however, this distinction makes little difference. **In fact, the difference in colour between heartwood and sapwood often adds a beautiful touch to wooden objects and can be used very creatively in everything you make.** Some wood species have particularly warm and beautiful colour shades and are therefore among my favourites, such as the shrink pot from yew in the photo. Other species have no heartwood at all and thus remain completely light in colour.

Although there are variations in that too, like the green shine in the wood of ivy. For wood preservation, which comes later, the type of wood can make a difference. In our forest, where the sapwood beetle is rampant, the sapwood of oak is affected very quickly. So, if I want to preserve oak to use the sapwood later, I bring it into our garden.

From a strength perspective, there is not much difference between heartwood and sapwood, but the heartwood is drier, often making it slightly harder to cut. This differs between wood species and also depends on when the wood was harvested. When cut in spring, the difference will be more pronounced than in winter, when the sapwood also contains less water.

The species that do form heartwood are called **heartwood trees.** Nice examples are oak, mulberry, robinia, plum, cherry, sumac, larch, Douglas fir, yew and redwood. Soft wood trees can therefore also have heartwood. Among heartwood trees, there are major differences in the time at which the formation of heartwood begins as well as in the final proportion of heartwood to sapwood. With American bird cherry, you can have twigs only a few centimetres in diameter of which half already have warm brown-red heartwood. On the other hand, it can also take a long time before heartwood is formed. In walnut, with its particularly popular dark brown-black wood inside, it can take decades, and the heartwood of ash is even more special. This takes 60 years to form, which is why it has its own name: olive ash. It is beautiful wood, as you can see in the seat of the chair in my workshop.

In some species, growing conditions can affect the amount of heartwood. Other species, such as robinia, are actually very consistent regardless of where and how they grow. Those trees always

photo. This phenomenon is caused by the reaction of a tree to attack by fungus. Cells and vessels are sealed off and substances are deposited in the wood tissue to stop the spread of the fungus. Those substances cause the discolouration.

have a few annual rings of sapwood, and the rest of the tree is heartwood.

In other tree species, there is dead heartwood, but no colour difference. This is caused by the absence of the extractive substances. Consequently, the durability of the heartwood is not better than that of the sapwood. Examples of these **trees** are beech and Norway spruce.

The last category is **sapwood trees,** which never produce heartwood, are less durable and usually also belong to species that do not live long. Examples are willow, alder, birch, poplar and maple. Hornbeam is also a sapwood tree, but is an exception in the list because of its hardiness and longer lifetime.

You may have occasionally seen wood with a nice core colour that, according to my overview, should not have core wood discolouration. This is possible. There is also wood with a **false core.** A typical example is the red core colour in some beeches or the different shades of brown to black in the centre of a poplar stem, as shown in the

GROWTH RINGS

The difference in early and late wood results in growth rings, but in ring-porous wood this colour difference is intensified. **Ring-porous trees** are species that produce remarkably more large vessels in the earlywood, sometimes even visible to the naked eye, but not in the latewood. Due to the grouping of the large vessels in the earlywood, the colour difference between light and dark annual rings is even more prominent.

Examples of wood species with this rare characteristic are oak, ash, robinia, elm and chestnut. These species are perfect for using the annual rings as decorative elements in your design. A nice example is this 'featherspoon'. This spoon is carved tangentially from a piece of robinia wood. By carving oblique surfaces in the handle, you get a feather effect that is enhanced by the shape of the handle. At the end of the chapter on the cooking spoon, you will find more information on tangential and other directions in which you can position your workpiece in the wood.

SMELL

The smell of wood disappears when the product is finished and the wood is dry, unless you cut or saw into it again. When cutting, the smell of some woods is really a fantastic experience. It is sometimes so powerful that it helps you identify the wood. It may seem an odd habit, but the first thing I do when splitting a log or branch is to smell the wood.

Many fragrances in wood are also used in all kinds of scented products and perfumes. **For me, the wood that smells best is without a**

doubt juniper: hard to describe, but a wonderful perfume! Fig smells like coconut milk, and if you detect a bitter almond scent, it's probably American bird cherry or maybe cherry laurel. Walnut smells like rich wet forest floor, and the sour smell of oak heartwood is so recognizable that, before even seeing it, I sometimes smell that an oak has been cut down somewhere in a forest. Personally, I love that smell. Cherry sometimes smells deliciously sweet, and apple or pear is always a surprise because of the many varieties. Eucalyptus wood smells as its name suggests. Beech, on the other hand, does not smell at all and is therefore often used for kitchen utensils.

BARK

Along with the wood, bark can help identify the tree. Many trees have a unique and recognizable bark, such as the spots in the bark of London plane, the white colour of birch or the warm brown colour of American bird cherry or Douglas fir. However, bark does not only differ between species, but also within the same species; a lot of variation can occur due to the age or location of a tree. For example, young birch branches are reddish-brown and later turn beautifully white, like the spoon in the photo. The bark of elder becomes coarsely cracked after a few years and then the typical pustules disappear. Boxwood becomes browner and more furrowed with age. Hornbeam becomes greyer with age and the slight cracks are reminiscent of an elephant's skin. The bark of young chestnut branches is smooth and in old chestnuts it is grooved, with the grooves appearing to twist around the trunk.

When making wooden objects, I regularly try to incorporate pieces of bark. On the handle of a spoon or on the outside of a shrink pot, bark can be really beautiful as well as emphasize the origin of the wood. There is a difference between species, but **the main reason why the bark sticks or not is the season in which the wood was harvested.** In full growth, the cambium is very moist and the bark loosens quickly. Willow branches can even be 'peeled' effortlessly in spring. In winter, the cambium is much drier and you can hardly pull off the bark or only remove it with cutting tools. Then the bark sticks to your spoon. The bark of walnuts is something special. It can become very thick and show beautiful dark shades through all the layers of bark and phloem. Hawthorn's bark is thinner, but has the same beautiful layers.

STRENGTH AND HARDNESS

For construction applications, there are many charts that describe all the physical properties of wood species such as tensile strength, specific weight, bending strength. You don't have to go that far for green wood working, but having an idea of the strength and hardness of the wood can help you choose the right type for a project. In the beginning, it may be more pleasant to work in softer woods such as willow, poplar or lime. With more experience, it becomes less difficult to work with harder types as well. Moreover, harder woods have the advantage that you can give objects you make a smoother finish. Strong woods also mean that you don't have to work as thickly to make a spoon or kuksa strong enough for its purpose. Some items like cooking spoons can take a lot of scraping and pushing at the front over the years. **If you want to make a cooking spoon that will really last a lifetime? Choose a hard type of wood.** For shrink pots or decorative objects, however, it makes less difference.

Beech and oak are tough, but even tougher and stronger are robinia or holly. Hawthorn and hornbeam can also be really tough. **The unexpected number one in terms of hardiness in our Belgian forests – and, in fact, especially in our gardens and parks – is boxwood.** It is a beautiful warm yellow wood that really shines because of its hardness when smoothly finished, like the cooking spoon in the photo.

The difficulty of processing wood ultimately depends mostly on the moisture level of the wood, which is actually the reason for working in green, fresh wood. The more moisture, the easier the tools pass through the wood and the easier the wood can be cleaved along the fibres. The difference is really big; think of biting into a freshly baked baguette versus sinking your teeth into a rock-hard, dry baguette.

Incorporating the hole into the handle made it a special eating spoon. The other photos show how sometimes when cleaving you find an ingrown twig in one half, while in the other you still have the hole where the wood has grown around the twig. If you make a spoon from both halves then you have a pair that always fits – an example of how spoon carving can even be romantic.

KNOTS AND NODES

A gnarl, node, knot, nub or knar are fancy, interchangeably used names for the transverse wood of branches that grow sideways and appear as round or oval discs on a board from the trunk. Transverse means you can see the ends of the wood fibres. If there are many knots, it means processing difficulties for the wood worker because of the harder wood. Wooden floors with knots are cheaper because many people consider this less valuable. A loose knot can be annoying though; when a branch dies and grows into the tree, the knot is in fact softer and looser, so the slice can eventually fall out. Then you end up with a hole in your floor or spoon.

In a tree, a branch has a different growth direction from the trunk of the tree. As a result, newer wood has to grow around this branch. The cutting direction becomes different – and unpredictable – in that part, and carving or cutting it is more difficult.

Even though working with wood with side branches has its disadvantages, **I embrace the imperfections, uniqueness and beauty of tree growth.** The spoons I made with knots are still the most beautiful to me. The first photo shows a freshly cleaved piece of walnut wood. There is a hole in it due to a side branch that rotted away.

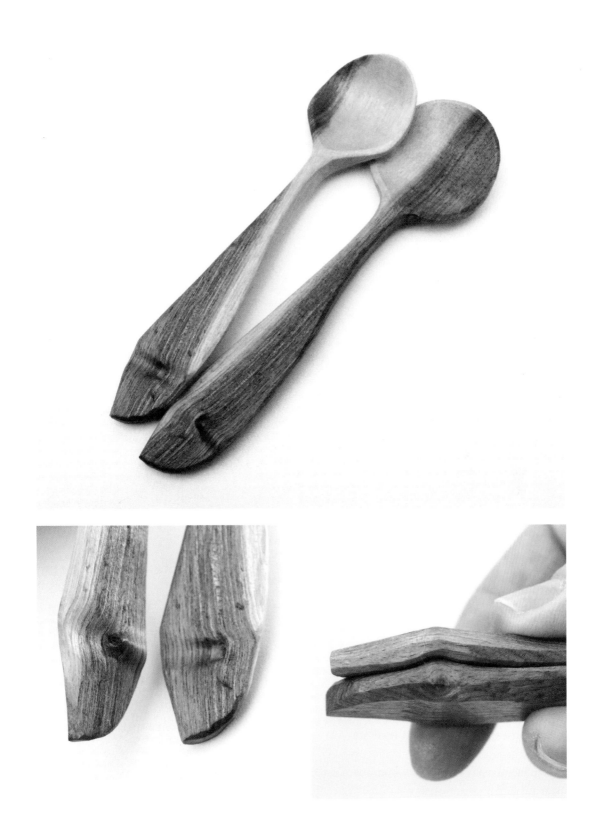

Wood and water

DRYING AND SHRINKING

Understanding how water resides in wood and especially how it disappears, will help you dry your kuksa in a controlled way, shrink your shrink pot or keep your stock of fresh wood moist for a long time.

Fresh or live wood contains a lot of water, but even the wood in our heated homes still contains moisture, just as there is always moisture in the air. To express the wood moisture level, we use the percentage of water in the wood in relation to the weight of kiln-dried wood. That wood is heated to 221°F (105°C). It stays in the kiln until there is no more weight loss and drying stops. A fresh 2lb (1kg) piece of wood that still weighs 21oz (600g) after drying contained 14oz (400g) of water when fresh. That means a moisture content of 66.6%, because 14oz (400g) is two-thirds of 21oz (600g). In living trees, the moisture content can vary from 30% to as much as 200%. The latter means that a piece of fresh wood, in weight, can consist of twice as much water as wood.

Drying is a gradual process from sometimes as much as 200% moisture to an equilibrium state of about 14% moisture in the air and a little less inside our heated houses. As wood dries, the percentage of water decreases. Eventually, the wood will also start to shrink. When the shrinkage starts, and how much it shrinks, depends on the type of wood and on the amount of free and bound water in it. The free water is in the cell cavities and is the first to evaporate when drying. No shrinkage occurs yet. It is not until **the bound water disappears from the cell walls that the wood will start to shrink.** For most wood species, this transition point is at about 30% moisture level. Compare it to a sponge. If you wring out a wet sponge, most of the water goes out, while the sponge keeps the same shape. You have pushed out the free water. If you let the sponge dry out further in the sun, it will eventually shrink and harden. That is the phase when the bound water also disappears.

Shrinkage is important for any wood worker. Wood shrinks in different directions. In the longitudinal direction of the fibres, shrinkage is negligible. This ranges from 0.1% as an average to only exceptionally 2% for young fresh wood or reaction wood. A 12in (30cm) cooking spoon will thus shrink less than a millimetre after drying. However, tangential and radial shrinkage do matter.

BEND OR CRACK

Tangentially (the red arrow in the direction of the annual rings), the wood shrinks an average of 10%. This causes cracks to appear during drying. Almost always they run to or from the heart of the trunk. This is partly because the heart of the tree has little strength and partly because the annual rings close to the heart are bent the most and the shrinkage therefore causes the most tension there. That is why we **prefer not to use the heart of the wood** in our carvings. If you cut a log in half, it usually doesn't take long for the first cracks to appear from the heart. Radially (the green arrow), the wood shrinks by half, about 5%.

Wood can therefore crack because of shrinkage, but mainly because different parts of a piece of wood have different moisture levels and/or dry at different paces. Transverse wood of which the cells are cut, will dry much faster than longitudinal wood, while wood at the surface also loses its water faster than deeper wood.

A fine, thin spoon will dry evenly, causing the wood to shrink but not crack. **The larger your**

carving or the more differences in short and long fibres, the more likely it will crack.** We can control this by slowing down the pace of drying and making it more consistent. Tangential shrinkage allows us to produce shrink pots, but it can also cause the bottom of your kuksa to bulge. Tangential shrinkage can be predicted because it appears as if the bent annual rings in the wood want to 'straighten out'. Radial shrinkage occurs perpendicular to the annual rings and can cause a radially cut tablespoon to become slightly narrower after drying. This is only a few millimetres, of course.

Even if your wood has cracks, you may be able to use this to your advantage. The surface of the cracked parts can sometimes be very organic. A good example is the spoon in the picture with the yellow handle. When I cleaved the wood along an existing crack, a special surface suddenly emerged that I could never carve myself.

If you **want to dry discs of end grain wood** – in which you can see the annual rings – it is very difficult, precisely because of the shrinkage and speed of drying in that end grain wood. Some wood species, such as catalpa, have a much

lower tangential and radial shrinkage of 4.9 and 2.5% respectively, which significantly increases the chances of success. Teak is the absolute champion with only 4% shrinkage, which is also one of the reasons for the popularity of furniture made from these exotic woods.

KEEPING OR MAKING WOOD GREEN?

Since we like our wood to be as green as possible for carving, you would ideally prefer to keep your wood moist for as long as possible. Or could we make wood wet or fresh again? **Wood is hygroscopic.** This means that wood can indeed absorb moisture again. It doesn't even need water to do so: it can absorb moisture from the air until the humidity is balanced again. This is the reason why you suddenly can't open a shrink pot that was standing next to the stove: the lid has absorbed moisture from the air and swelled inside the pot. Wood can absorb moisture again and swell, making it slightly easier to carve. But it never gets completely fresh and soft again like live wood.

As wood dries, it is important to think about the size of your stock. Here are **some practical tips on how to slow down drying:**

Keep the wood moist for as long as possible. A log will start drying at the cut ends. It takes a long time for the inner wood to dry as well. A 6½ft (2m) log can be still green in the middle a year later.

Wood dries when laundry dries well too: when it is warm and windy. **Store it in a shady and sheltered place outside.**

You can seal the end fibres to slow drying. Leftover wood glue, paint or beeswax work well.

Cold slows down the drying process. Moisten the wood under the tap and put it in a plastic bag in the fridge. After a few days, mould may start to grow, though, so change or air the bag regularly. For the longer term, the freezer is therefore better. Here, the plastic bag protects the wood from freeze-drying.

The bark serves as protection for the tree and **also slows down drying,** so leave it on as long as possible.

If, after these tips, you still have beautiful pieces of wood that are completely dry, it is great to give them a second life in tool handles, in jewellery or in the lids and knobs of shrink pots.

Wood and fungi

BEAUTY AND DECAY ARE NEVER FAR APART. This is all the more true when it comes to the very complex relationship between trees and fungi. They can live together in perfect harmony. But fungi can also kill trees (parasitic fungi) or clean up fallen trees (saprotrophic fungi). Thankfully. What would a forest look like if every fallen tree remained there forever? The relationship between fungus and tree is a fundamental part of a forest's ecological system.

Fungus is the collective name, with sometimes negative connotations, of a very large group of organisms. Under the right conditions, **fungi form fruiting bodies that we know as mushrooms,** but some are barely visible. Fungi reproduce via spores. In every breath we breathe in countless spores: they are everywhere.

Wood is roughly half cellulose (sugar chains) and a quarter lignin (filler). Depending on which substance is preferred, fungi can be divided into the types of rot they cause. These substances are sometimes the reason for a true war between the tree and the fungus. This results in **the beautiful discolourations in the wood, as silent witnesses, of a battle on a microscopic scale.** As a collective term for these discolourations, wood workers often use the word 'spalting'.

We can sometimes see the discolouration as black lines in the wood. These are **zone or demarcation lines** and indicate the boundary where a fungus holds out against the tree's defence mechanisms or against another fungus that is also engaged in the war. As defence, the tree starts to store extra protective extractive substances in its cells to stop the fungus. These dark-coloured zones with faint outlines are called **reaction zones.** These discolourations can occur separately or together. The lid of the shrink pot in the picture is made of horse chestnut. The black lines make the pale wood that much more special. The serving bowl is made of pale, white maple wood. The dark half is a fine example of a reaction zone. But where the reaction zone stops, you often see the demarcation lines of the mould as well.

Not all discolouration is caused by fungi. Bacteria can also cause abnormal colours. Sometimes it is difficult to identify even for specialists. **For us wood carvers, it is mainly a source of fantastically beautiful wood.** The following

Demarcation lines

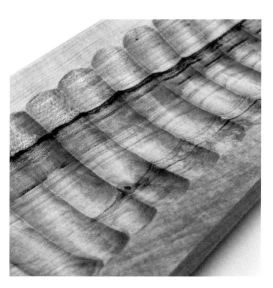

Reaction zone

photos show two more examples of discolouration that I cannot explain. The top of the handle of the spatula is discoloured cambium that I have preserved. In the other two spoons, just the edge of the handles have the heart of the wood, which had started to rot due to a crack in the branch.

I often leave wood lying in the forest or wait to fell a tree until fungi are clearly present in the wood. Sometimes I split the wood too early and there is very little to see. Sometimes I am too late and the wood rot has progressed so far that all the strength is gone from the wood. But sometimes I am perfectly on time. Then, I try to **honour** the beautiful **wood by turning it into something special.** If you don't have time to work with the wood immediately, a freezer will inhibit the mould; cooking the wood is also fatal to fungus.

Most fungi also cannot continue to live below 20% humidity and certainly not at 14%, as is often the case in our air. **Therefore, spoons or pots with discolouration do not pose any problem or risk.**

A special parasitic fungus is the beefsteak fungus, which especially likes the tannic acid in oaks. The fungus looks like a bloody steak and is edible, although not very tasty, in my opinion. In oaks, the fungus causes a very unusual brownish-red discolouration of the heartwood after a few years. I have inserted wooden dowels with traces of the fungus in an oak in the Spoonforest that has to be felled for forest management purposes. Unfortunately, I have to wait a few more years to know if it has succeeded. How exciting it will be to split that wood for the first time.

WOOD IN A NUTSHELL

Where to find wood?

TREES GROW JUST UNDER THE BARK, SO DAMAGE TO A TREE IS AN OPEN DOOR FOR FUNGI AND BACTERIA. This is why you should never just cut off a branch.

Although at first glance it may seem difficult to get fresh wood, after some detective work you will soon have enough. **Above all, let your neighbours know that you are looking for wood and why.** You can also consult arborists and gardening companies, the waste collection station or the local gardening service. If you see someone sawing wood in the garden, stop by and you might get lucky. If you come here to the Spoon Club, you will always have plenty of wood.

I am lucky to have my own piece of forest, which means I have sufficient supplies, but not all wood species grow there naturally and forest management has priority. Having my own forest allows me to go through the whole process from tree to finished product. A very special journey along different skills, tools and tasks. If you have a garden, then you can also start planting! After all, an old Chinese proverb says: *the second-best time to plant a tree is now, the best time was 20 years ago.*

03

CHOP, CUT, SAW

The carving axe

I AM AN AXE MAN. I don't quite know what that means exactly, but at least I have a thing for axes. I love axes and I still find it hard to imagine how I spent the first half of my life without one. I am exaggerating a bit, but **I use an axe almost every day** and it still does something to me every time I pick up the axe and work with it in wood. For many people, an axe is something from grandpa's garden shed or a medieval weapon of the Vikings of the north. But very often I notice that once people learn to use an axe, it very quickly feels like a natural, sharp extension of the arm. I never had anyone on a course who really couldn't handle the axe. From 14-year-old girls to an 86-year-old man – in the end, everyone has fun swinging an axe in their own way. Often beautiful to watch! I think the reason for this is to be found in our historical relationship to the axe, which goes hand in hand with the history of mankind and the use and processing of wood in our past.

HISTORY

A 10,000-year-old axe was different but still very clearly an axe. The first axe, if we don't take a fist axe into consideration, was made when a piece of flint was processed to get a sharp edge then mounted on a handle of wood or bone. Man – and his ancestors – had been working flint for millions of years. It seems that **the axe with a handle was only used for the first time after the last Ice Age, around 8000 BCE,** in northern Europe. Flint is a hard rock that is usually found in layers in limestone. That is why the coasts of Dover and Cap Blanc-Nez are full of it. Flint can be broken and worked in such a way that it has hard and very sharp edges at the same time. So hard that when you hit a piece of pyrites or iron, you get sparks. The iron is scraped off and the friction generates heat; together with oxygen, you get sparks. So, the iron generates the sparks and not the stone.

After stone axes came axe heads made of copper about 5,000 years ago. Later, they were also forged from bronze and iron, and very recently – in the last 300 years – from different types of steel. Thanks to the availability of ever better and stronger materials, more and more different types of axes are also made for different applications: from a small 14oz (400g) wood carving axe to a cleaver with a head weighing several kilos.

When the axe was most popular in our culture (i.e. before there were chainsaws and other sawing machines), there was an axe tailored to and suitable for every job in wood. The axe was at its height in the 18th and 19th centuries in America, where dozens of companies manufactured different types of axes.

Many jobs of the past are no longer relevant in our society today and tools have been replaced by machines, but the wood carving axe is still being made and improved.

Today's axes are the optimal result of human evolution and its technical ingenuity in constantly improving tools to make our lives easier. But still an axe is so beautiful in its simplicity and natural in its use. I don't remember me or anyone else ever wondering how to hold an axe or what it is used for. It seems to be embedded in our culture and history, and thanks to its use by people like you and me, it will remain so for some time to come.

SAFETY

Many trainees are not so familiar with using the axe as a precise cutting tool, as opposed to a knife, which we hold in our hands every day. I often notice that trainees have a healthy trepidation about the axe and, on the other hand, are sometimes too confident with the knife.

I have never hurt myself with an axe; at the most a few cuts by grasping the axe head and not paying attention to where I put my hands, or even once when grinding when I was rushing. In all these years of teaching and workshops, there has only been one person who injured himself and needed a few stitches. This confirms that the tips and safety rules below are important and, above all, really work. Sometimes I notice that trainees look at my hands at the beginning of the day and some of them say outright that they check whether I still have all my fingers. You lose fingers by working with heavy sawing machines, which is something for joiners and carpenters. **Green wood working is a very safe hobby or job despite all the sharp tools!** Really!

Never forget these **three safety rules!**

POSITION OF THE WOOD ON THE CHOPPING BLOCK

It seems obvious, but when starting to use the axe it sometimes feels like you have to think of many things at once and then you might forget about it. We use a chopping block to chop on. That can be a low block where you have to sit, but a high block on legs is better in my opinion and really worth putting time or money into. If you can work standing, you are more mobile and your back is straighter and less stressed than if you sit. A block serves as a support for your workpiece, of course, but also as a stop if the axe goes through the wood. **You want the axe to end in your chopping block** and not next to it, ending up in your leg, for example. Put your workpiece at least in the middle of the block or preferably a bit to the back. Don't put it at the very front or on the side where you chop.

KEEP FINGERS OUT OF THE CUTTING SURFACE/PLANE

None of the fingers of the hand holding the workpiece – referred to as the wood hand – should be in the area or at the side of the workpiece you are chopping. Humans have an opposable thumb, just like monkeys, but human thumbs are stronger and more flexible than our other fingers. So, we can stabilize a block of wood and also handle an axe easily, which would be difficult for apes. Therefore, **the thumb should not be within the cutting plane.** The tips of the other fingers may also be in the area, which we want to avoid too. So, how should we hold it? It depends on the size of the workpiece and may vary as the chopping and carving progresses. Fortunately, we have flexible hands and can thus avoid the axe ever going into our other hand.

03 DON'T CHOP TOO HIGH

As a rule of thumb, **avoid chopping in the top third of the workpiece.** If you want to chop off a piece in that zone, turn the piece upside down to make sure this zone is at the bottom. This way we avoid reaching very high with the axe where it might hit our other hand. However, sometimes there is no other way because of the cutting direction, but then I hope an alarm bell rings in your head alerting you to the fact that you are reaching high and this is potentially dangerous. The solution is to bring your wood hand as far to the other side as possible and only let your axe cut into the wood with small wrist movements while holding the axe very high on the handle (see left).

As your experience grows, you may feel that these rules are less necessary, as you can chop more and more precisely and accurately. But even experienced axe men and women can get tired or momentarily distracted. When I make spoon blanks, i.e. do axe work on spoons, the axe might go up and down 1,000 times in a day. The rules are there to avoid cutting yourself just that one time when you were not paying enough attention.

USING THE AXE PROPERLY

CUTTING WITH THE AXE

With the axe, but also for example with a knife, plane or drawknife, it is much more efficient to use a slicing cut instead of pushing the tool through the wood. Read the piece about 'slicing' on the right to learn more.

Slicing

Slicing is a basic principle when working with any kind of cutting tool. The best way to explain this is to use the example of a tomato. You need to cut a tomato in the kitchen and you have a sharp knife in your hand. What happens usually when you put the knife on top of the tomato and push the knife down? Exactly: the tomato is flattened and eventually cracks. That's not what we want. The solution is to 'saw' with the knife, i.e. move it back and forth to pass it through the tomato. When we use a tool with a sharp, even cutting edge, we don't call this sawing but slicing. If you use the entire length of the edge – or at least more than just that one contact point – when you push, the knife cuts through the tomato much more easily. The mathematical principle behind this is that when cutting at an angle, the angle of the tool's cut reduces as it passes through the surface, thus experiencing less resistance and cutting better and more efficiently.

What goes for the tomato also goes for cutting in wood. With any tool, always try to use the entire length of the edge – or at least as much of it as possible. This not only makes cutting easier, but also improves the result, namely a nicer or flatter surface on your wood. Cutting in wood has a lot to do with technique and the right cutting motion and much less with strength or calluses on your hands.

To maximize the cutting effect of the axe, you need to make the right movements. For some, these come naturally, for others it may take some practice. Before you read on, you might want to film or watch yourself in the mirror and pay attention to exactly which muscles you are using and what movement the axe head is actually making. **The best movement comes from a combination of elbow and wrist.** Your upper arm hardly moves, but your forearm goes up and down. Combine this with your hand, which also goes up and down, and with the axe, which is somewhat loose in your hand. So, from a 'loose wrist' and without clamping the axe.

The movement starts with your upper arm hanging beside your body, forearm up, the wrist tilted upwards and the axe loosely in your hand bringing the axe head as close as possible towards your upper arm. The movement ends with your upper arm still in the same position, forearm down and the wrist tilted forward. The

combination of these movements causes the axe head to actually describe a quarter to half of a circle. Chopping like this ensures that the axe enters the wood at the bottom of the edge; the **circular movement uses the entire length of the edge** and the axe exits the wood along the top of the edge.

What you shouldn't do is raise your shoulder and try to push the axe straight down through the wood. In that case, you not only have less power, you're also using only a small part of the edge. Then you are not slicing. Later, when you've got this all figured out, you can also use your shoulder to increase the force and size of the circular shape of the forearm and wrist movement, but that's very different from lifting the shoulder.

Placing your thumb on the handle of the axe is not a good idea. That reduces the circle and thus the slicing motion of the axe. The axe can only be

tilted back as far as the thumb allows. With some experience, you can loosen the grip on the axe, cutting even more (without letting go of the axe, of course). If you feel quick cramps or pain in your hand or wrist when working with the axe, it usually means you are holding the axe too tightly. Of course, your muscles need to get used to the movement and physical work. But **to cut properly with an axe, muscle strength is really secondary.**

SMALL OR LARGE SWINGS

Chopping or cutting with the axe is done in a (part of a) circular motion. The position where you hold the axe handle also affects it. If you hold the handle at the bottom, you automatically increase the rotational movement and generate more power. However, more power and speed often implies less precision. If you want to work more precisely, aim better or cut more safely at the top of your workpiece, it helps to grip the axe halfway or even completely under the axe head. This reduces the swing, and if you only use the wrist rather than the elbow, you get the smallest cutting movement possible. **The more experience you have with the axe, the less precision and speed become each other's opposites.**

ODE TO THE LEFT HAND

Those who are just starting to carve with an axe often assume that the right or dominant hand does all the aiming and power work and that the left or other hand is only there to hold the wood. Nothing could be further from the truth. **Wood carving using an axe is a creative interplay of both hands!** The right hand will steer and allow the axe to cut, but the angle or direction from which the axe enters the wood is the responsibility of the left hand. With the right hand, you always swing the axe from top to bottom. That way, you let gravity help, you build up muscle memory, you can easily see from above where you are chopping and you can therefore aim best. Your left hand tilts the wood so that the axe lands in the right place and at the right angle. More simply put, the right hand takes care of the almost machine-like movement, which is as efficient and even as possible, and also determines the power. The left hand is the designer who puts the piece under the axe in such a way that the wood is chopped away where needed and something beautiful emerges.

A common mistake or misunderstanding of the left hand is when you put the workpiece on its flat bottom so it is more stable. As a result, the right hand also has to do the creative work, which it is less good at. You will eventually start to bend your body, which is exhausting and reduces precision. A good example is how you chop the round shape of the bowl of a spoon. If all goes well, the right hand does the same thing all the time, but the left hand will tilt the wood a little more with each stroke of the axe resulting in a nice round shape, just the way you want it.

PARTS OF THE CARVING AXE

Since I want to give my students the chance to work with axes from different makers, brands and price ranges, I have the perfect excuse to buy a new axe regularly. A good wood carving axe has a number of properties that often also determine the cost, in addition to the amount of handwork it took to make it. I like to explain these important properties below using one of my favourite axes, that of Hans Karlsson, a Swedish blacksmith.

THE HANDLE

The handle of an axe is usually made of American hickory or European ash wood. Both species have the best strength-resilience ratio due to their long elastic fibres, making them excellent for stems and handles. At the same time, they are strong and can absorb shock well. Although these types of wood are optimal, I have also worked with axes that had handles made of birch or oak, for example, that performed equally well. The handle of my favourite axe is made of elm, not quite as good as ash, but nicer, if you ask me. The impact that a wood carving axe has to endure is not the same as that of, say, a large splitting axe. The type of wood therefore matters a little less, but length does. Most wood carving axes have a handle between 8–16in (20–40cm). With a longer handle you can work just as well and precisely, but the balance will be more to the back. This is more tiring for your hands. Also, the handle can get in the way of particular grips or positions. The longer the handle, the greater the swing you can take and the more power you can apply. However, it usually comes at the expense of precision. This is exactly why some people prefer shorter handles, which automatically allow you to work more precisely – but then the balance is often a bit more forward.

I prefer the golden mean of about 14in (35cm). Short enough to hold the axe high to do fine work and long enough to hold the handle at the bottom and hit hard when there is still a lot of wood to be removed.

The balance or balance point of an axe varies. It depends on the weight of the axe head and the weight and length of the handle. Ideally for me, the balance point is where you hold the axe for fine carving, just below the axe head. That means your axe is nicely balanced at that point; you don't have to use any extra muscle power to keep the axe straight and you can focus all your energy on carving.

The curvature you see on the underside of the handle ensures that when you hold the axe more backwards, your hand doesn't slide off the handle. That can be dangerous. I prefer the handle in its transverse section to be shaped like an aeroplane wing: oval with a rounded side and a slightly sharper side. The rounded back feels pleasant in your hand and the slightly sharper front helps when aiming the axe.

Some axes have a hole at the bottom of the handle to attach a string. I don't understand why that would be necessary, unless you are an itinerant woodsman who can use the string to attach the axe to the outside of his backpack.

THE EDGE

This is where wood carving axes differ most from other axes. First, there is the angle of the cutting edge; that is the enclosed angle of the two bevels that meet in the sharp edge we are chopping or cutting with. For a carving axe, I prefer to have that angle around 25–30 degrees. That is similar to a wood carving knife. Many axes have a thicker edge and are thus sturdier, but also do not cut as easily and are better for cleaving or heavy felling. Learn more about this in the chapter 'Swiftly smart sharpening'.

Another difference is the curvature of the axe's blade. The more curvature, the more the axe's cutting motion is emphasized. You know by now: a longer edge extends the cutting. So why not a very long and curved edge? Then again, the axe head would become so large and heavy that the balance would be more forwards and less comfortable or precise to cut. A really good wood carving axe is the best average of both advantages.

NOTCH IN AXE HEAD

A recess or notch just behind the edge at the bottom of the axe head allows your hand to hold the handle just behind the cut. If you combine this with an upright position having your eyes in the same line as your axe and your workpiece, you can aim and cut very precisely. Thus, you can see very well what your axe is doing and evaluate and possibly adjust with each stroke. So, this is the ideal position for very fine axe carving.

The notch can also make the axe head lighter and improve the balance point, but besides balance, the overall weight of the axe is also important. To me, the ideal weight is between 21–28oz (600–800g) for the overall axe. My first really good axe was the carving axe by Gransfors. At first glance, it has all the good characteristics of a carving axe described above, while being made of recycled quality steel and forged from start to finish by the same blacksmith, who puts his initials in the head as a sign of his craftsmanship and the quality of the product he has made. However, the weight of the total axe is 35oz (1kg). I am a sturdy guy with quite a lot of arm muscles, but if I use this axe for a long time, I get tired faster than using a slightly lighter axe. With a 21oz (600g) axe, I can swing all day.

Then again, I think a 14oz (400g) axe is too light. Gravity helps to swing the axe down, but if it's so light, you constantly have to add extra force to the swing, resulting in less precision or you have to swing a lot more to have the same effect. However, my body may work differently from yours. I hope the above helps you find the ideal axe for you.

WHICH AXE TO CHOOSE?

The information I have given about axes is meant to explain the difference between a wood carving axe and other types of axes and also explains why some axes cost arouond £200 or more and some only around £40. Do I mean that you really need an axe that has the best of all those features or characteristics? Not at all! In its essence, wood carving is about technique, knowledge, practice and creative fun. Compare it to a car. Any decent car gets you from A to B, safely and within the same time. Just as you can make a beautiful spoon with any decent axe. But if you want to travel to the south of France by car – to carve a nice spoon under an olive tree – then a car with air conditioning, cruise control, seat heating, hyper-sophisticated ultimate handling, multi-functional digital radio and so on will get you there just a little more comfortably and pleasantly.

By a decent axe, I do not mean a cheap axe from the DIY shop. Those serve for all sorts of things except for carving, mainly because of the blunt cutting edge-angle. The axes I sell are reasonably priced and cost around £80. Ultimately you decide what you like to spend your money on and how often you will use the axe. Wood carving is my profession and I sometimes do it for many hours a day, so I have a very ordinary car, but lots of nice and especially good axes.

The wood carving knife

IF YOU HAVE BEEN GIVEN OR BOUGHT THIS BOOK BUT HAVE NO
EXPERIENCE IN GREEN WOOD WORKING YET, chances are your interest
was triggered by the special appeal of wood or by **the special feeling of a sharp
knife and the desire to create something with it,** or a combination of both.
During the basic workshops, I often ask why people came to me. Very often the
answer is about wood, the forest, a branch, a knife and the youthful desire or
memories of using a knife to create something from a branch. I will build on these
memories and offer new ways to make something beautiful with a knife. I myself have
a very vague memory of a trip where a boy and an old man sat together on the side
of the street and carved figurines with a knife. The austerity of that image is in huge
contrast to the wonderful figures they were carving from the piece of wood. That
image never left me.

Like the axe, the knife has a history as old as mankind. From a sharp piece of flint to a contemporary carving knife. The difference is not so great when you consider that there may be a million years of evolution between them. **A knife is perhaps man's most universal tool of all times and cultures.**

Unlike the ideal wood carving axe, the knife is much plainer and less specific. The blade's bevel usually has an angle around 25 degrees; the length and shape can vary and the handle can have many shapes, but comfort is the most important consideration.

So, what is the difference between an Opinel – a French pocketknife – or a genuine Rambo knife? After all, both allow you to sharpen a stick. What Opinel is in the world of pocketknives – affordable, frugal and solid – the Mora knife from Sweden is in the world of wood carving knives. The massive and machine-made production of this knife and its simplicity result in a very decent knife for around £25.

CHARACTERISTICS

The thickness of the blade is a primary difference from other knives. The thickness of Opinel pocketknives or potato knives is thinner than the $\frac{1}{10}$–$\frac{1}{8}$in (2.5–3mm) of most wood carving knives. The first reason is that a potato knife is too thin for certain techniques or cutting in hard wood and might break, especially at the tip. Secondly, the cutting edge is also different and to achieve that 25-degree angle with a Scandinavian grind, a wood carving knife also needs a certain thickness (see chapter 'Swiftly smart sharpening' for more details). Thicker than $\frac{1}{8}$in (3mm) is not needed for ordinary wood carving. The default length is 3–3½in (7–9cm), which provides for a relatively long slice that allows a good cutting motion. Shorter blades are also handy, especially with very small workpieces where your wood hand comes close to the blade and you are therefore less likely to prick or cut yourself with a smaller blade.

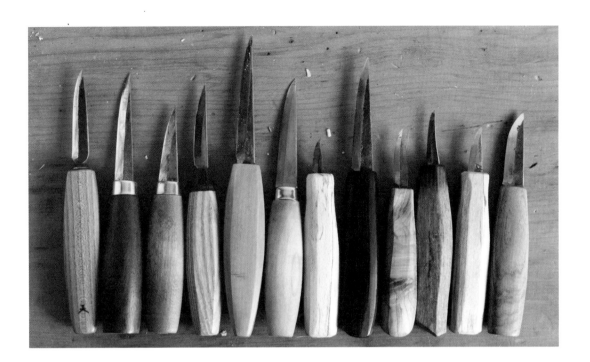

The long narrow tip is specific to a wood carving knife. The tip is particularly interesting if you want to cut short curves. If the blade is too wide, the side would collide with the edge or corner in the wood preventing you from making the curve. Only with the upper part of the narrow tip is this feasible.

Besides the Mora knife, there are many other brands and makers of wood carving knives. Some are a lot more expensive than the Mora knife, but rarely really much better. Sometimes they are made of a better type of steel and the knife is slightly harder, which means that its sharpness is preserved longer. You can also find knives with a smaller angle of cut, which makes them slightly sharper, but more fragile at the same time.

If your budget is limited, I would opt for a low-cost wood carving knife and spend a bit more on the axe or one of the other tools that I talk about later in the book.

Personally, I think it's special to make my own knives – for me or by request from other people. Not the metal blade, but the handle and sometimes the leather cover. In my workshop, I have a large collection of special, beautiful pieces of wood of all kinds. Many handmade knives I buy do not yet have handles. I love designing and carving beautiful handles for them. The black knife in the photo, for example, is made of 5,200-year-old bog oak originating from the Blankaart in Diksmuide, Belgium. Isn't it special to hold a piece of wood from a tree that grew at a time before the Egyptians started their pyramids? Since it was under water for such a long time in the peat without oxygen (and thus no rotting) and due to the chemical reaction of the tannins of the oak with the acidic water, the wood turned pitch black. Had I found this piece a few million years later, it would have been coal. This knife does not make my carvings better or more beautiful. But it is a special feeling every time I hold the rare black wood in my hands, sometimes for hours a day.

SAFE CARVING

When it comes to safe carving with a sharp carving knife, there are two old Flemish sayings that need to be challenged. When I ask trainees what is good advice for working safely with a knife, I often get the answer to cut away from you. I will show below not only why it can still be dangerous to cut away from you, but also why cutting towards your body can be totally okay. **Cutting safely with a knife starts with understanding the movement of the knife exactly:** where does the movement start and where should it end. So, it depends on the muscles that are used during cutting and how the movement ends.

During my workshops, I often need a few plasters, but nothing serious has ever happened with a knife. This is largely due to the safety tips below, but also due to the fact that I feel responsible during workshops and always position myself where I can see everyone with a turn of my head. From experience, I can see very quickly which position, movement or challenge in carving could be potentially dangerous. Usually, I can correct participants or instruct them in time.

If you, dear reader, pick up your wood carving knife all excited later, I won't be sitting next to you, so I would ask you to read through the tips below carefully and really make yourself familiar by practising. Should you end up cutting yourself, I hope it's no big deal and that you understand why it happened. A student once had the idea of decorating his spoon with red dots of blood. Fresh blood is a beautiful bright red, but unfortunately it soon turns brown, so you don't have to do it for the colour either.

Another misconception is that blunter knives are more dangerous than sharp ones. The logic behind this statement is that a blunt knife

requires more cutting power and gives less control when the knife slips through the wood. For untrained hands or those who are unfamiliar with the grips below, I can agree. **However, if you know how the grips work and what to do to cut safely, then slipping is sometimes part of the technique and therefore not a problem.** From experience, I know that a razor-sharp knife that can cut large pieces of wood with power faces little resistance from a bit of human skin.

Some wood carvers like to work with protective equipment such as metal-reinforced gloves or leather finger guards and the like. On the one hand, this makes me miss the feeling and connection to the wood and I cannot carve as precisely; on the other hand, you also become more dependent on those protective devices and experience less what is safe because you always count on that protection. Would you still like to use protection?

> **Just a few final tips or obvious ones that we still sometimes ignore:**
>
> - If you are tired or restless inside, it is probably better to put down the knife or other sharp tool and relax for a while or continue reading this book.
>
> - Alcohol and carving is really not a good combination!
>
> - Do not leave a knife or other tool unattended and always use the cover when you take a break or stop carving.

SIX KNIFE GRIPS

A knife grip is a way to hold your knife and cut. There are six basic grips – with a few variations – that I use every day. These are certainly not all the possible grips, but if you master these you can create everything from this book, and much more. I only use other grips very sporadically. I focus on the grips that you really need and complement each other well.

In addition to the description of the grip and necessary photos, I shall go into detail on four topics: safety, cutting (see box on page 58), application of the grip and possible variations. The descriptions are extensive, because the details are often important. Sometimes people do something for years without realizing what a particular grip is really for or why it just doesn't work so well. Some grips feel more natural than others or require more or less practice. Hang in there. **Every grip that you master increases the pleasure of wood carving and improves the result!**

If this is completely new to you then it is a good idea to practise the grips with a soft fresh branch, say an inch thick and the length of your arm. This way you can focus on your grips and your own safety without worrying about the end result. It is useful to know different grips that you can alternate. That way, you bring **variety in the use of your muscles.** This reduces fatigue and spreads the load across different muscles.

01
FORWARD GRIP

If you have ever cut a sharp point to a stick at the campfire to roast marshmallows or sausages, then you probably used this grip. With your knife hand, you cut forward, away from your body. In its basic form, this grip begins with the knife on the wood and a bent elbow. The forward power comes from stretching the arm. For extra power, the shoulder and even the back and abdominal muscles can be used together. The knife cuts through the wood and when the knife exits or the piece of wood is cut completely, your hand will shoot further forward until your arm is fully stretched. If your knife is stuck, you have cut too deep and tilted your knife too much in the starting position. With every grip, it is a search for this balance to find the ideal initial position or tilt angle of the knife that allows for a viable and efficient cut: not too small, not too big.

Safety. Since this is a powerful grip where the blade can slide out as far as the swing your hand can make, there is a large area where you don't want to hit yourself or anyone else. Despite the fact that this is a cutting motion that moves away from you, if you cut down while sitting with a straight back, you can hit your own leg. To avoid this, you can cut sideways, next to your legs. Or even better: bend forward putting your elbows on your knees. Then your legs will always be safe. Using this grip, it is also important to be aware of others around you. Especially if a right-handed and left-handed person are sitting next to each other, they can easily get into each other's cutting zone. Perhaps very obvious, but make sure your wood hand is not in the area where you start cutting.

Cutting. You can transfer maximal power to the knife if you start cutting as close to the handle as possible. However, if you then push the knife forward in a straight movement, you are not cutting efficiently. Instead, try moving the knife outwards while cutting. The slicing cut starts close to the handle and the knife exits the wood at its tip. This way, you use the entire length of the knife.

A common intuitive position is to put your thumb on the back of the handle. Don't do that: your thumb is not as strong as your wrist. When cutting you need power to get the knife through the wood. The resistance of the knife in the wood allows your wrist to bend inwards. You want to keep your wrist at least straight and when you put your thumb on the handle, all power comes from your thumb and not your wrist.

Application. The forward grip is a very powerful grip that you often use at the beginning of your carving. This is when you need power to cut large pieces of wood. Precision is less important at this point. However, the grip can only be used when you can slide out freely and there is no other part of your carving in the way to suffer unwanted cuts. So do not use this grip to cut from the handle of a spoon towards the bowl.

Variant: shoulder grip. This grip relies more on shoulder strength and bending your back. While sitting, you cut next to your legs on the side of your knife hand, but while standing, you can generate more power. Keep the elbow stretched right from the start. Since the cutting movement is more difficult with this grip, you need a sharper cutting angle. To do this, tilt the knife a little back from the start. Hold the knife firmly and push it through the wood using your shoulders and back muscles.

02
THUMB GRIP

This way of cutting forward requires the thumb of your wood hand to push the back of the blade of the carving knife. As such, the movement is limited to the range of your thumb. Unlike the forward grip, your knife hand or arm does nothing in the forward direction. If you practise this grip, you will notice very quickly that it allows you to make small but very controlled cutting movements. It is important that the thumb of your wood hand comes to the other side of your workpiece and thus pushes on the back of the knife somewhere in the middle or close to the handle. You are more likely to cut with the pointed part of your knife. It is better not to place your thumb directly over the part of the knife where you are cutting, as the wood will get in the way of pushing properly.

Safety. Because the movement of the blade covers only a few centimetres, this is a very safe grip. Do not use your cutting hand or arm in this movement, as this will result in a forward grip. The only times I've seen someone cut themselves using this grip was either because they put the workpiece and their hands in their lap and the tip of the knife hit their leg, or because they brought the index finger of the wood hand too far forward to hold the wood and that's exactly where the tip of the knife ended up. Perhaps you should try these two unsafe situations to see clearly what I mean – and then avoid them from now on.

Application. This is primarily a finishing grip that makes small and very controlled cuts on almost any part of your wood. But beware: for starters this safe feeling can also be a pitfall. Sometimes you switch to this grip too quickly and it can take a very long time to remove wood. With any of the other grips, it would be faster. The only limitation

71

CHOP, CUT, SAW

is that the shape or size of the workpiece should allow your thumb to reach the other side of the workpiece and push the back of the blade.

Cutting and variants. I describe both together here because this variant of the thumb grip allows for more of a slicing motion and thus uses a larger range of your knife. In the thumb-pivot grip (the child must have a name), you keep the thumb of the wood hand extended and still, but in the same place as the regular thumb grip. However, the movement now comes from the knife hand being tilted or rotated backward, with the knife pivoting on the thumb. This way, you may not be able to use the full length of your blade, but more than when you are pushing using the thumb grip.

Once you are more familiar with both variants, you will not only move the thumb when pivoting to obtain a smaller or larger turning angle, but you will sometimes combine them. This involves both pushing and pivoting; that way, you can still make a longer cut in a very controlled way. I have a fairly rigid thumb, but I have seen spoon carvers who start these grips with the thumb pulled all the way back and then can push it forward for as much as 4in (10cm).

Its name is self-explanatory: we are going to carve just like peeling potatoes (at least as in the days before the vegetable peeler was invented). This is a grip where we cut towards the body. However, the movement is limited because it starts with the fingers opened as far as possible (but still holding the knife) and ends when your hand is completely closed. The only body part you can encounter in this short distance is your thumb used to counter the push. This grip is of course limited in power because you only use your fingers, but still a lot more powerful than the thumb grip because all your fingers work together.

Safety. The biggest difference with peeling in the kitchen is that wood is harder than a potato. This makes the movement less predictable. Your knife can suddenly slide through the wood. So, don't put your thumb in line with the knife movement! You have to hide your thumb or put it around the corner, for example behind the handle of your spoon, to ensure the knife ends next to your thumb when accidentally sliding out. The difficulty is that many people have to unlearn rather than learn something: they often forget to bring their thumb into a safe position. I once saw someone who not only squeezed their hand using this grip, but also reinforced the movement with his arm. This is dangerous and completely different from the potato grip.

Cutting. For small or short pieces, you simply pull the knife through the wood. If you want to use the potato grip to remove longer, larger pieces, you need to slice instead of pull. By slicing you reduce the power on the wood. When cutting at right angles to the fibre, this ensures that no wood breaks out at the end, or at least it's less likely. To slice, start with the edge on the wood close to the handle. While contracting your fingers, turn the piece of wood up or your hand down (or a combination of both). This ensures optimal use of the cutting edge of your knife. So, this is actually a kind of pivoting movement around your thumb.

Application. The peeling grip needs the thumb to counterforce the movement of the other four fingers without being in the trajectory of the blade. That means this way of cutting works well on the ends of a stick or workpiece: in positions where, because there is wood in between, the thumb can be put down safely. What is also special is that the peeling grip is the only grip where the hand – and thus the knife – can make a rotating movement, allowing you to partially follow the curve when the shape is convex. With the forward or thumb grip, you automatically cut straight ahead or sometimes make hollows.

Variant: the can opener grip. The big advantage is that you can apply this grip if you can't get your thumb away safely with the peeler grip. The principle is the same. Your thumb gives counterforce and your cutting movement starts with the knife facing you with an open hand and the other four fingers holding the knife. The big difference is that the force or movement does not come from the fingers or the hand that is closed, but from the wrist and forearm turning upwards with the thumb as the pivot point. The thumb pushes the top of the wood and the rest of your hand pivots up as the knife cuts through the wood. Where or when does the movement end? As you cut upwards, at some point your index finger meets the wood and the knife can't go any further. That is the safe stop of this short but powerful grip. Cutting is automatic, because you start with the tip of your knife, and by turning up, you end with the part close to your handle.

Variant: can opener grip

04
CHEST GRIP

This grip reminds me of my grandmother pushing a loaf of bread against her chest and then taking a slice of the bread with a knife, thus cutting with the knife towards her. This grip is similar, but has a few key differences. With your wood hand, you grab the wood at the back and push the other side against your chest. With the knife, you start at the back, the edge facing yourself, and pull the knife through the wood towards you. This way, you can cut long pieces in one go. You use long and flat strokes, where you have a lot of control and can clearly see how you are carving.

For control, it is important that you press your upper arms against your body all the time! When carving, your hand comes towards your body with the knife and your elbow goes back a bit, but then your forearm remains in contact with your body. I personally like to put the thumb of my knife hand on the side of the blade, but you can also just make a fist.

Safety. The danger of this grip is not where you would expect it. If you slide through the wood while pulling the knife towards yourself, the blade will never hit your chest. Rather, it is your fingers that hit your chest and stop the movement. If you try to cut in such a way that the tip comes towards you and you hit yourself while sliding out, you'll notice that the elbow of your cutting arm has disconnected from your body, in which case you lose control and the power to cut properly.

What you need to watch out for with this grip is your wood hand! The most important advice is: keep your knife upright when you cut, i.e. with the tip upward. This way, you can follow the path of the knife – and watch closely what you are cutting – and you won't hit the other hand. If you

put the knife down or horizontally onto the wood, you risk hitting the palm of your hand, just below your thumb, on your wood hand when carving. An inconvenience with this grip is that your chest or sternum may start to hurt if you push the wood against your chest for a long time or if it has sharp parts. To prevent this, you can put a piece of leather with a string around your neck which will take most of the pressure away. If you keep using this grip – or are careless like me and keep losing that bib – you will naturally grow calluses on your sternum after many hours of carving. You won't even feel it anymore when you push the tip of a stick against your sternum.

Cutting. With the chest grip, you can use the full length of your knife by starting to cut close to your handle and pulling the knife down as you cut towards you. With some practice, you can direct the movement in such a way that you reach the tip of the knife exactly when you also reach the end of the section you want to cut.

Application. This way of cutting allows you to make long cutting movements on straight pieces or to cut an inside curve on curved pieces. Your eyes are relatively close and you look at your workpiece from the top (unlike, say, the forward grip), which means you can constantly monitor and adjust the shape you are carving. Although you can use a lot of force in this way of cutting, 'slipping' is limited and controllable by tilting your blade slightly backwards and thus playing with the reach of the grip, because you know it stops when your hand reaches your chest. This is why this grip is great for cutting the handle of a spoon, for example, where slipping would mean your knife cuts into the bowl.

Variant: the reinforced chest grip. To push the wood against your chest, you only need your index finger and maybe your thumb. The remaining three fingers can add extra power

when cutting by putting them onto the fingers of your other hand and pushing them along in the movement. The range of this help is limited, of course, but you can also move your wood hand slightly towards your chest, cutting bit by bit with the support of your wood hand.

Another variation is to use the three fingers of your wood hand as a pivoting point allowing the knife to make a rotating movement towards you, which again allows you to cut more at a short distance than if you were to pull the knife through.

THE CHICKEN GRIP OR THE SCISSOR GRIP OR CHEST-LEVER GRIP

For many, this is the most difficult or least 'natural' grip. I had to practise this one many times, but once you master it, it becomes one of the most important ways to cut! You can get it wrong or do it just a little differently in so many ways, which means you don't benefit from the advantage this grip can provide.

To get the right cutting position, bring your hands to your chest and hold both the knife and the wood facing up in your hands. This means that when you open your hands, the knife and wood remain in your open hands. If they were to fall down then you are holding them incorrectly. The knife lies on top of the wood where you want to start cutting; your thumb on the blade, the edge away from you. **Your forearms are pressed firmly against your chest.** The essence of this grip is that you start with your shoulders brought forward; the movement comes from pushing your chest forward and pulling your shoulders back at the same time. Your forearms pivot on your chest. This way, knife and wood automatically separate, like a scissor movement.

Your wrists and arms don't actually do anything except for holding the wood and knife firmly. The power of this grip is greater than any other grip. You use your shoulders and chest, which generate greater force than your hands or arms. Therefore, it is necessary to raise your hands almost uncomfortably high, at the level of your chest or preferably even slightly higher. To clearly feel or understand the difference: try doing the same with your hands at the level of your abdomen. You can move your chest or shoulders as much as you like, the knife won't go anywhere.

Safety. The grip ends automatically when your arms cannot pivot further around your chest. This way, there is actually little cutting risk with this grip. The only times I did see someone cut themselves, they either brought their hands together too impetuously, causing the tip of the knife to poke into the other hand, or the wood hand came too close to the point where they started cutting.

Slicing cut. Again, if you start cutting with the part of the blade closest to the handle, you will automatically start using the rest of the blade due to the scissor movement. The longer your blade, the greater the slicing motion you can make.

Application. This grip is similar in application to the forward grip. It is more powerful, also shorter, but it does not slide out. This grip is ideal to powerfully cut away a lot of wood, though the cutting length of this grip is limited to the length of the blade. You look on top of the piece you are cutting and not to the side, which would make it harder to see what shape you are cutting. Although your eyes are close and with some practice you can cut in a very controlled manner, this is mainly a brutal grip to remove a lot of wood quickly.

Variation. You can also cut by turning outwards with your wrists – or just the wrist of your knife hand. Or you can pull your wood backwards and hold your knife firmly. These variants make sense thanks to the control you have because your forearms are firmly pressed against your body, and because you are cutting close to your eyes. They are especially suitable for finer work. These are fundamentally different grips because you are not using the strength of your chest and shoulders.

Perhaps this is not a true grip like the rest because you are not cutting away wood but cutting or severing fibres. Although this grip rarely appears in books, it is very useful for decorative carving. So, I thought it was also important to come up with an appropriate name. The principle is simple: you put your knife perpendicular to the wood and as you push down hard, you also move the knife back and forth. This wiggling up and down movement generates just a little more cutting action than if you just push the knife into the wood. As a result, the cut is also deeper.

Safety. Although I have never cut myself using the wiggle-wiggle, I think it would be wise not to do this above your legs, should you ever slide out next to the wood.

Application. You can make a cut across or straight through the fibres without cutting the workpiece completely. It is a stop cut in combination with another grip. The other grip is used to carve towards the cut made by the wiggle-wiggle. You can easily stop there because the fibres are already cut. So it's ideal to use it in combination with the thumb or chest grip.

Variant. Actually, none, but for deeper notches, you might be better off using a saw.

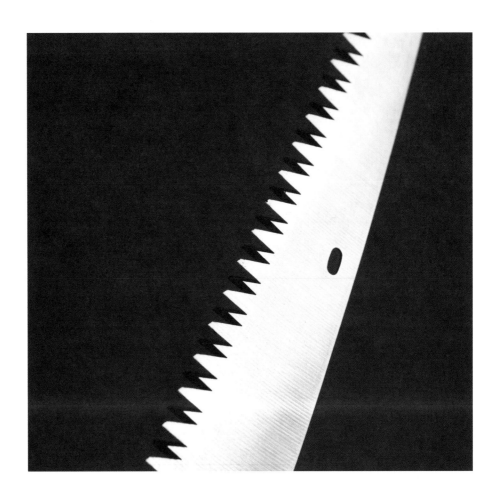

CHOP, CUT, SAW

The (pull) saw

YOU CAN WRITE AN ENTIRE BOOK ON DIFFERENT TYPES OF SAWS AND THE HISTORY OF THE SAW. Every application does have a specific type of sawing tool. Although much sawing is now done with machines, the hand saw still has a fundamental place in the wood workshop or the spoon carver's backpack. This book is not about dovetails or complex and sophisticated Japanese wood joints, but a saw is also indispensable for the green wood worker.

First, there is **the crosscut saw,** for cutting across the fibres of wood. A thin branch a few centimetres in diameter might be cut with one swing of the axe. But as the pieces become thicker, the saw simply works better than the axe. If a 12in (30cm) oak trunk needs to be cut in half, I always opt for the saw. By better, I don't just mean that you need less force or time to cut through the wood, but also, for example, that the amount of wasted wood is significantly smaller. With a saw, you make a fine cut as wide as the saw teeth; with an axe, you have to carve out a V-shape and lose much more wood.

Secondly, there are **saws that rip.** These cut in the direction of the fibres. Axes or cleavers are the masters of longitudinal wood splitting, but unfortunately, they can't stop at a certain depth. For that purpose, you need a rip saw.

Rip saw

Crosscut saw

FEATURES OF THE PULL SAW

Before we take a closer look at sawing, I will explain the difference between Japanese pull saws and our western saws, which saw mainly when pushing. For me, the choice was made long ago in favour of the pull saw. Although my handmade wooden frame saw is one of the most charming tools I have, a pull saw has many practical advantages for me.

A pull saw cuts only when you pull the saw towards you. In the push movement, where you push the saw away from you again, nothing happens except that you bring the saw back to make another pulling and sawing movement. The teeth of a pull saw are therefore always slightly tilted towards the handle. When you pull, you need to push the saw down at the same time to make the teeth 'bite' or saw into the wood.

The main advantage of a **pull saw is that it can be thinner and lower in height** than a push saw. Thinner means cutting less wood to get a log in two. Lower height implies the saw is less likely to get stuck. It means that less power is needed and it is faster. This also reduces the need to clamp your wood firmly; you can use these saws more easily while just holding the wood with your other hand.

With a pull saw, you must **not apply power downwards** when **pushing** because the saw could get stuck, bend and eventually even break. Compare it to putting new laces in your shoes. First, you push the tip of the lace through the hole. Once you can grip the tip, you pull the rest of the lace through the hole. Why not push the whole lace through the hole? A lace bends easily, which makes pushing it difficult. Exactly the same thing happens with a pull saw. It is very thin –

less than $\frac{1}{32}$in (1mm) in some fine pull saws – and therefore flexible. **When you pull the saw through the wood, the rest of the saw automatically follows.**

A disadvantage of extra thin saws is that it is a bit more difficult to make nice and straight cuts. A thicker western saw that bends less will automatically ensure a straight cut. With a pull saw, you have to start more carefully and pay more attention to keep it straight. Of course, there are also pull saws with a reinforced back that keep the saw straight. But that thicker back in turn limits the cutting depth.

Pull saws are lower in height, so they are **easier to fold.** This is handy to carry in your backpack. And because a lot less steel is needed, they also remain affordable.

The last big difference is the hardness of the teeth. Western saws have the advantage that the teeth of the saw are not as hard and therefore can be sharpened. However, setting and sharpening saw teeth is a craft in itself and requires a lot of experience and practice. The teeth on pull saws are so thin that they have to be made extra hard otherwise they would bend too quickly. Some teeth have a hardness of up to 68 HRC (see the chapter 'Swiftly smart sharpening'). That means **rock hard and too hard to be sharpened.** The advantage is that this means these saws stay sharp for a very long time. The disadvantage is that if they get blunt over the years, you have to replace the saw blade. Many brands of pull saws take this into account and offer the blades separately from the handle.

With both pull saws and western saws, you often have a choice of how many teeth per inch you want. **The more teeth, the smoother, or the less fraying remains after cutting.** If your saw simply serves to shorten a branch, you're better off with fewer teeth. This saw cuts coarsely but faster. If you saw a log for a shrink pot, for example, with a fine saw, the surface is already so smooth that it does not require any finishing later. If you only have one saw then – as is often the case – the average is good for everything.

Most saws have teeth that alternate at the bottom of the sawing blade and are sharpened on the inside like knives, with the edge in the cutting direction. These serve to cut crosswise and cut fibres. Rip saws look very different. The teeth resemble a row of chisels, which easily cut wood in the direction of the fibres. You can do some ripping with a crosscut saw too, but it's really much easier with a rip saw.

SAFE SAWING

Of course, we never want to cut, chop or saw into our own body. In that respect, saws have an additional disadvantage compared to cutting tools: **the wounds are very rough and heal slower.** The few scars on my hands that are still visible were from a saw, mostly from accidentally holding the saw in an incorrect manner.

Some words about a fantastic but dangerous invention, the chainsaw, are appropriate here. This is one of the machines I use often, and although my big pull saw also goes through wood quickly, the chainsaw makes the job so much easier and faster. Especially if, for example, I need to cut a large log into pieces for a workshop weekend making bowls for ten people. **Make sure you have good training and equipment if you are going to work with a chainsaw.** It usually goes well, but trees and wood are sometimes unpredictable and wounds from a chainsaw are terrible. Fortunately I am not speaking from personal experience, but I always try to be very focused when using a chainsaw.

Western framesaw

Bending the saw

If you have little experience, it is recommended to keep your wood hand as far as possible from the cutting position. **If you can clamp the wood, your wood hand is completely safe.** With a small piece of wood, you sometimes have no choice but to put your wood hand closer, in which case it is extra important to **start slowly**. If the saw is not really in the cut yet, it may jump up and hit your wood hand. Once the cut gets deeper, you can increase the speed or push harder.

You can also control the power of a pull saw depending on where you hold the handle. If you hold the handle close to the teeth, you will automatically apply less force. Conversely, if you hold the handle at the back, you will automatically push or pull harder.

However, the most important thing, especially with pull saws, is to **move the saw through the wood as straight as possible.** If you move it at an angle, the saw can clamp, break or jump up. When I saw very attentively, I'm looking much more to the saw than to the wood, checking that it is moving straight.

Finally, you need to slow down just before you completely pass through the wood. As you push downwards when pulling, the saw may in fact slide out towards your legs when it exits the wood. With some practice, sawing becomes as easy and smooth as chopping with the axe or carving with the knife. There is no need to be afraid of any of these tools. But **healthy caution, practice with the above tips and focus are always important.**

Happy carving!

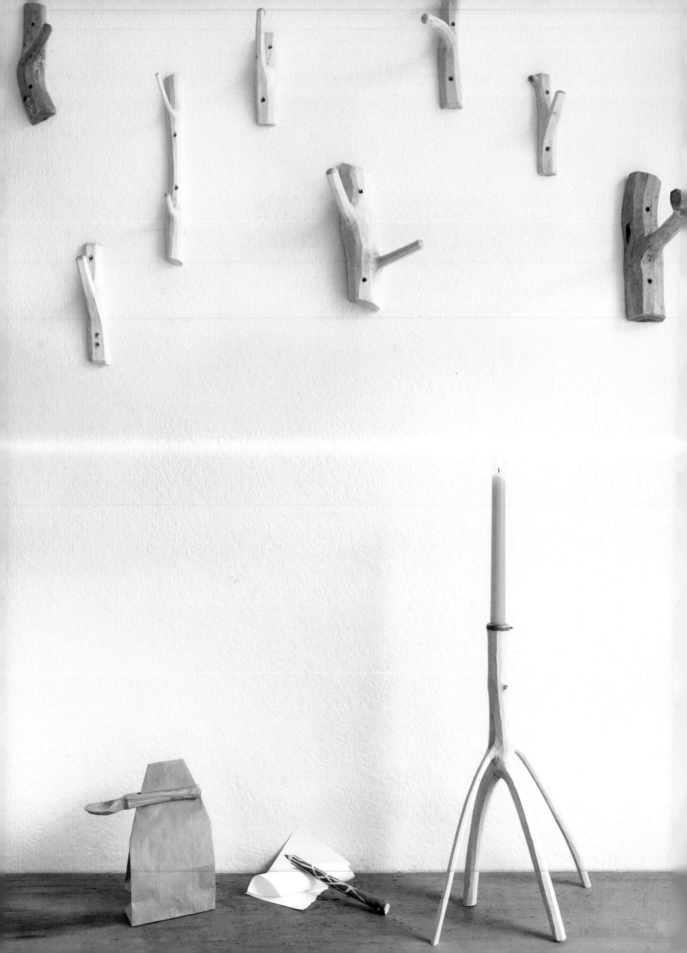

04

FROM TREE TO TABLE

FROM TREE TO TABLE

Going with the grain

BEFORE WE DIG IN AND APPLY WHAT WE'VE LEARNED ABOUT WOOD AND THE USE OF THE AXE AND KNIFE, we need to take a look at **the concept of cutting direction.** When cutting or chopping wood with sharp tools, you need to be aware of the direction. The correct direction is always with the fibres or with the grain of the wood. This means that if you cut in the opposite direction, the wood may crack at worst, or the fibres will not be cut properly resulting in a rough surface. Some students understand very quickly which direction they should cut in, but many others keep on struggling with it, sometimes leading to frustration or even failed carvings. For me, determining the cutting direction is something I rarely have to think about. Nevertheless, **during the design phase I do contemplate the impact of the shape on the cutting direction,** but this is more and more intuitive.

Wood is actually a collection of strong fibres and vessels in the longitudinal direction of the wood. These fibres are composed of cells, which mainly consist of cellulose and lignin. These are the most common types of organic material on our planet. Lignin is primarily responsible for the strength of wood. If force is applied along the lengthwise direction of the fibres – e.g. with an axe – especially when it's fresh, the wood will split easily along the fibres. **However, if you try to make an oblique cut through the fibres, you will feel resistance.** The reason for this is that your tool has to cut through several layers of cells, which **can be done in two directions.**

To illustrate this, I tape a bundle of sticks together, as a reasonable representation of how wood is composed. When chopping a bevel, it can be done from the side inwards or from the bottom (or top) outwards. You might expect that both methods have the same result, but that is not the case at all.

If you paid close attention to the safety instructions in the previous chapter, you'll know that starting at the top is not a good idea with the axe, but that is not what we are focusing on right now.

When chopping from the side inwards, the axe will first hit the outer sticks, which represent the fibres. A sharp axe passes through the fibres easily, but the lateral force pushes the outer fibres inwards. Since underneath those fibres are other layers of fibres, they cannot be pushed inwards. They stay in place and the axe cuts through without too much trouble.

If we try to chop the same bevel from the bottom outwards, the direction of the force applied to the fibres is different. The axe enters on top of the sticks (fibres) and the force moves outwards. This means that the fibres that first come into contact with the axe are pushed to the outside. Since there are only a few fibres between where the axe starts and the outer edge, they do not stay in place but are bent outwards. As a result, the fibres are broken rather than being cut properly. Furthermore, the axe can end up between the fibres and cleave rather than cut. What will actually happen is determined by the applied power, the type of tool and the amount of wood that is cut incorrectly. A knife (which cannot apply the same power as an axe) is unlikely to cleave the wood, but may get stuck between the fibres, or partially break and cut the wood. This might result in a surface of broken fibres, rather than a smoothly cut surface.

How to remember? We always cut from the outside to the inside. Or, depending on your view, from top to bottom or from thick to narrow. You can draw an imaginary line in the centre of the object, a bit like the middle stick in the whole bunch, then always cut along the direction of this line.

Can you cut along the fibres lengthwise? An axe will cleave the wood like this, but chopping actually starts with a crack in the wood. How that crack continues depends on the fibres and is not determined by the axe. Even with a knife, you can never cut perfectly along the fibres. We cannot see the different layers of cells with the naked eye and they are rarely perfectly straight. Therefore, you always have to cut diagonally through the fibres.

If you are having a hard time finding the proper cutting direction, it helps to pay attention to what happens while cutting. **Using the axe, you will notice too late that the direction is wrong,** ending up with a cracked piece of wood. Sometimes, you can cut in the wrong direction

with a knife without realizing. Take a good look at the surface left after cutting. It should look shiny and feel smooth. **Fibres standing, broken pieces, scratches in the wood...they usually indicate that you were cutting in the wrong direction** (or that your knife really is blunt).

How should you do it if you want to cut completely transverse or perpendicular to the fibres? The first answer is that you might be better off using a saw. Cutting across is much trickier than cutting diagonally and is not easy with an axe or knife. However, if it improves the smooth finished surface of your workpiece to cut transversely with the knife, remember to cut from the outside inwards up to the middle. Cut the other half in the opposite direction. If you don't do this, the last fibres may deflect outwards or eventually break.

You can mitigate the risk by using a very sharp knife and using a slicing motion. It reduces the impact of the knife on the wood and the chance of breaking.

Using an axe, you can mitigate the risk of fibres breaking on the outside by having the outer fibres supported on your chopping block, which prevents them from bending outwards and breaking. With a warped shape, however, it can be difficult to support the wood in the right place.

FROM TREE TO TABLE
Wood

AS INITIAL PROJECTS, WE CARVE DECORATIVE OBJECTS OR UTENSILS TO USE IN THE KITCHEN, ON THE TABLE, AT THE CAMPFIRE.... In each finished product, you can still recognize the origin of the wood (the branch itself).

Cosy rustic or clean-cut and modern, there is a flavour for everybody. These are relatively easy projects to be made from a branch with few tools; and with a little creativity, they become real eye-catchers. In how many products in your home do you still recognize the raw material, the base product or the origin of the material? Simplicity is a virtue; and these are good exercises to start with to master the tools and the different knife grips. Trainees often tell me that from a walk in the forest, they brought a special branch with the intention to create something from it. This chapter was written especially for these people and those branches.

COAT HOOK

A unique coat hook in the hallway or in a room can already be an eye-catcher, but a whole set adjacent to each other makes an entire room special. Carvings can be sober and quick or, on the contrary, graceful and elaborate. For those who like to be creative with painting techniques, finishing possibilities are endless.

THE WOOD

Find a stem or branch that has one or more side branches. The diameter depends on what you want to make; 3–4in (8–10cm) is perfect. Any type of wood is suitable, but I prefer to use soft wood as it cuts more easily. One exception is holly. Although holly is harder, due to its growth in the forest (under taller trees), it often has many side branches very close together, which allows you to create a coat hook with up to six side branches. The fresher the wood, the easier the carving. When harvested in spring, you can remove the bark easily. Without cutting, just by peeling off the bark, you obtain a natural pure look.

FROM BRANCH TO COAT HOOK IN 6 STEPS

01 **Saw the branch to the desired length.**
Keep in mind that there should be enough wood above and below the side branch to drill holes to mount the coat hook on the wall. You don't want the holes on the edge either, to avoid cracks when drilling.

02 **To remove the back of the branch,** you can use the axe and cleave (a nice, straight branch) or chop (a bent branch) to the heart of the wood. This reduces the risk of cracks after drying and immediately produces a flat back that fits against the wall. Flattening the back perfectly is not an issue at this point. During the drying process, the branch may bulge a little. You will fix this only after drying. When cleaving, the idea is not to take a swing with the axe and hope you aimed well enough to land exactly in the heart of the branch. Put the axe in the right place onto the branch and hit the head of the axe with a wooden club (see box on page 94 for how to make one) or a heavy stick. **If the axe cleaves through the wood,** it may slide out next to the chopping block. Obviously, you don't want this to happen and wound your legs. Therefore, **hold the axe perpendicular to your body so that it exits sideways and not towards you!** If the cleaving result is not straight after all (e.g. due to a twist in the branch), you can fix it with the axe. For rounding the top and bottom, I also chop away most of the wood with the axe.

03 **Saw the side branches to length.** If there are several side branches above each other, it is practical if the top ones protrude. This way, the garment at the higher position will hang above the lower one. You can vary the side branches of coat hangers from 1–12in (3–30cm). Let your imagination run wild, but above all, take into account the room where the coat hook will live.

04 **Cut the desired shape into the coat hook.**
You can round the edges or the end of the side branch so the garment slides over it easily. A ball on the end is also nice and useful. You can leave parts of the bark or remove it all. The possibilities are endless. Carving a hanger is sometimes odd or difficult to hold, which is precisely why this is a good first exercise to practise the knife grips safely.

05 Drill two **holes in the coat hook for the screws to mount it on** the wall. Take the diameter of the screws into account; $^5/_{32}$ or $^3/_{16}$in (4 or 5mm) is usually sufficient. You can cut the edges of the drilled holes to recess the screw heads. You can also use special countersink drills for this purpose. For a refined finish, you can cut a round piece of wood to size after tightening the screw and glue it into the drilled and countersunk hole; this way, the screw becomes invisible. To do this,

you need to drill a hole in two steps. First, you drill about $^3/_{16}$in (5mm) into the wood with a $^3/_8$in (10mm) drill. Then, drill further into the same hole through the wood with a $^3/_{16}$in (5mm) drill. Screw the screw all the way in and cut a round piece of wood and glue it in the $^3/_8$in (10mm) hole to make the screw head invisible.

06 **Let the coat hanger dry for a few days.** If necessary, you can flatten the back a little.

MAKE YOUR OWN WOODEN CLUB

A club is a very useful tool in your collection and easy to make yourself from a thick branch or trunk.

The wood

Find a 12–16in (30–40cm) long branch with a diameter of 4–6in (10–15cm). The heavier the wood, the longer the club's lifetime. **Oak, ash and robinia are ideal types of wood,** but birch or chestnut are also suitable. Preferably use a straight piece of wood that is nicely rounded at the lower end, as this will become the handle. For a more durable beater, use a piece of wood that has side branches or knots in the upper end. The transverse fibres will provide for a more durable head, but it is not necessary.

At the bottom of your log, draw a circle representing the thickness of the handle. For my hands, I like a thickness with a diameter of 1⅜–1¾in (3.5–4.5cm). Measure the distance from the circle to the outer edge. Now, you need to **cut** this deep in the middle of **the log,** all the way around. Find a way to measure the depth of your cut so that you don't cut through the handle. If you have a deep saw, draw a line on the saw to indicate the depth you have to cut to.

Turn the branch upside down, the handle pointing up and, **using an axe, cleave away the parts next to the circle** of the handle. Of course, you don't have a club to do this at this point, but any heavy piece of wood will do (although it won't be as easy to hold as the solid club you're making). Stay away from the edge of the circle to make sure that any crack you make will definitely stop at the cut. If you cleave 'behind' the cut your club will split into two pieces. Once some parts have been removed, you will get a better view of the depth of your cut and you can continue to cleave, or **chop away** the **last parts with the axe.** If necessary, saw deeper here and there. When your handle starts to get shape and thickness, you can **finish** it **nicely and smoothly with a carving knife.**

BAG CLIP

To properly seal a bag of crisps, biscuits, coffee and the like, to keep it fresh for longer, you can create a very handy clip from a branch. Clothes pegs used to be made in the same way.

THE WOOD

A twig about 1in (2.5cm) thick and 4–6in (10–15cm) long is perfect. **The part that will clip the bag is preferably as straight as possible.** The handle may be crooked or gnarled, whatever you like. Looking for the ideal branch for this? Then **hazel** is the easiest: soft but strong wood. Especially the new shoots growing out at the base of the bush, which are exceptionally straight with few side branches and have long pieces of equal thickness. It is also very suitable wood for making arrows and spears.

FROM BRANCH TO CLIP IN 4 STEPS

01 Before splitting or sawing the branch lengthwise, you need to **drill a hole.** The reason for this is that when you use the clip, you open both sides which may cause the split to crack further. A ³⁄₁₆in (5mm) hole is enough. Drill straight through the branch to ensure you go through the middle on both sides.

02 Secure the branch in a vice or with a clamp in order to **saw it lengthwise from the top to the hole.** Sawing is slow and controlled. Using a rip saw will make it faster since you're sawing along with the grain, but with an ordinary saw it also works. Another option is to split the branch by placing a knife on top of the branch and hitting the back of the knife with another stick. This provides less control and you need some luck to get the crack to end exactly at the hole.

03 To get a bag into the opening more easily, it is important to widen the first ³⁄₈–³⁄₄in (1–2cm) and **enlarge the opening slightly.** You do this by cutting outwards (with the grain) with your knife using the thumb or potato grip.

04 The rest is up to you to **refine or decorate** the clip. If you used a fresh branch, the split can open up a little more after drying. To prevent this, clench the split with a rubber band and it will remain closed even when it's dry.

CANDLESTICK

Although many types of mood lighting exist, real candlelight is still special and atmospheric. Especially when the candle is placed in a hand-carved, unique candlestick. It can have a cosy place somewhere in the living room or be a central showpiece in the middle of a beautifully set table. This is an easy little project, but the challenge is to find the right piece of wood.

THE WOOD

If you watch how bushes and trees grow while walking in the forest, you will see that a branch has a side branch every few centimetres. Ideal for coat hangers, then, but **for a candlestick we actually need at least three branches or legs that all grow diagonally upwards, close together and spread around the main branch.** So you need a branch that grows crooked, turning the main branch into a leg, while it has two side branches in the right place. Another possibility is a branch that splits into three, which is even rarer.

Most likely you will find a suitable candlestick branch **in an old hedge.** These plants are often pruned early in their growth, leaving a main stem that branches off in different directions. The branches divide with each pruning. It is as if the shrub keeps making new branches to try to outwit the pruner. Every plant wants to grow and pruning wakes up the dormant buds and the plant will start to produce a new branch. If you cut off a frequently pruned hedge plant at the bottom and turn it over, you are likely to find a beautiful candlestick branch. Keep in mind the desired size of the candlestick and make sure the main branch is thick enough to hold the desired candle.

FROM BRANCH TO CANDLESTICK IN 5 STEPS

01 Once you have found a suitable branch, **cut** the main branch and three side branches (legs) to remove the candlestick from the tree or bush. Leave some extra wood on the main branch and the legs and try to cut the legs at about the same length, so that the main branch is more or less straight when you put it on its legs.

02 Since we are only going to do some superficial trimming of the main branch, leaving the heart of the wood, there is a risk it might crack. The question is whether you want to get started immediately or take the time to dry **the branch slowly** and reduce the risk of cracking. Especially when you remove the bark, the branch will dry out faster and therefore often show bigger cracks. If you don't want to wait and don't mind about cracks, a metal candle holder (or 'candle cup') can help secure a candle well and firmly in the split main branch. Keep the extra length on the main branch as long as possible, as you might be able to cut away most of the cracks that way.

03 As with the other branch projects, you can keep it very basic when cutting the candleholder or **go** all the way **in decoration.** *Have fun!*

04 The size of the hole you need at the top obviously depends on the kind of candle you want to put in. The easiest way to make the hole is by drilling. Drill deep enough to ensure the candle sits tightly in the candlestick. Be mindful that an unattended candle can fall over, drip wax or even set your house on fire. **Use a drill as close as possible to the candle diameter and trim the remainder with the carving knife.** If you only have a few millimetres left on the edge, then chances are that the branch will crack when drilling. In that case, you can make a series of holes with a smaller drill while finishing it with a chisel. The area at the bottom does not need to be finished smoothly because you won't see it later anyway. **A metal candle holder can be decorative, but also has a number of other practical advantages:**

• Without a candle holder, the sides of the main branch need to be thicker to avoid breaking when pushing a candle into the hole; with a candle holder, the metal provides the strength.

• It is difficult to finish the hole nicely with an ordinary wood carving knife. The candle holder hides the inside and also part of the top edge.

• If you have a big crack in your main branch, a candle holder ensures you can still use it.

• Adds an element of safety by separating the candle from the potentially flammable wooden part.

05 Finally, you need to **saw off** the legs nicely in order **for the candlestick to stand straight, and supported by all of its legs.** To do this, put your candlestick on a flat surface and tuck packers under the legs where needed to make it stand straight. Now, put a pencil on a plank at least as thick as the thickest object you used to raise one of the legs. At the same height, mark all the legs all around and saw on the lines. I use the same method to cut the legs of my stools, chairs or chopping blocks to length.

99

POT HANGER

I made a pot hanger for the first time during a bushcraft course in England. Each time it's super fun, especially if you enjoy cooking on the campfire from time to time.

The pot hanger is a bit of an odd object in this series and, in fact, there are much simpler ways to hang a pot over a campfire. Nevertheless, the basic design combined with the mechanism to connect both halves makes **this pot hanger ingenious in its simplicity.**

THE WOOD

Find **two similarly shaped branches, each with a side branch** that can be used as a hook. We will connect the long parts of the main branches, while one hook will be used to hang the pot and the other to hang the whole on a branch above the fire. The main branch should be as straight as possible towards the end (on the opposite end to the hook). For a strong pot hanger, it is best to choose **a strong type of wood** and a side branch that is (preferably) as thick as the main branch.

FROM BRANCH TO POT HANGER IN 8 STEPS

01 **Cut the hook to length** and saw the main branch just underneath the hook. Make sure there is enough wood left where the side branch enters the main branch to keep it strong enough.

02 Put the branches side by side, with the longer parts overlapping. The hooks should point outwards on both ends. **Use your wood carving knife to mark where one branch ends on the other and vice versa.**

03 Where the mark is made, **use the wiggle-wiggle to cut deeper into the mark.** With the

thumb grip, cut from the end of the branch towards the mark. Do this until you almost reach the middle of the branch.

04 **Using the forward or scissor grip, carve away the rest of the wood** from the mark to the end. Try to keep the surface as straight as possible. Do this with both branches. When you are done, **both ends should fit together nicely.** If they don't make contact in either direction, you have to shorten one or both branches, or move the first mark further and cut away some more wood. The better they fit, the more likely the connection will be strong in the end.

05 Now, you need to **cut out another angled piece** starting at the mark towards the hook of the branch. The angle of the cut-out part should be 45 degrees (or smaller). Again, both parts should fit together as perfectly as possible and make contact with each other everywhere.

06 Finally, **carve a slot** in the middle of the cut-out section, in the same place on both branches. To do this, put them side by side to mark both with a knife or pencil. In this case, the marks are 2in (5cm) apart. Again, use the wiggle-wiggle cut to cut the marker lines to about ⅛in (3mm) deep and remove the wood between the marks with the thumb grip.

07 Both ends are now ready. To complete the clamping system, **make a wedge** that clamps into the slot. Cleave, saw and chop a piece of wood that is just over ¼in (6mm) by 2in (5cm), and about 4in (10cm long). Use your knife to further refine the wedge and make the front just a little smaller so it fits into the slot and is completely fixed halfway.

08 The wedge pushes both parts open, but as they fit together nicely, they cannot separate. Your pot hanger is ready.

  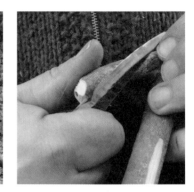

FOREST PENCIL

This is a project with very simple steps, but with some practice you can create the most beautiful pencils. I enjoy making them, but the grateful amazement of children getting them is a good enough reason to mention them here. Sometimes I feel like carving something, but don't have the time or space at that moment to make something that requires more tools. Then, I take my pocketknife, find a twig and get to work.

In its simplest form, you drill a hole in a straight twig and insert the pencil lead – and you're done.

With more time and eagerness, you can add decorative carvings or letters or other shapes. If you use fresh wood, you can drill the hole 1/64in (0.5mm) wider than the pencil filling. This ensures that the fragile filling slides easily into the hole, and it will be fixed inside thanks to the shrinking of the branch later, without the need of glue.

The only thing that can be a challenge is finding pencil fillings that are thick enough. I use refills with a diameter of 1/8–1/4in (3–6mm). As a finishing touch, you carve a sharp tip – and your pencil is ready.

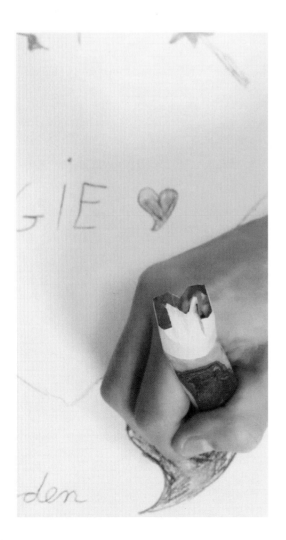

Good workmanship, that is careful,
considerate and loving work,
requires us to think considerately of the whole process,
natural and cultural, involved in the making of wooden
artifacts, because the good worker does not share the
industrial contempt for 'raw material'.
The good woodworker loves the board before it becomes
a table, loves the tree before it yields the board, loves the
forest before it gives up the tree.

Wendell Berry

05

BIG SPOON, LITTLE SPOON

BIG SPOON, LITTLE SPOON

Spoon carving

MY GREEN WOOD WORKING JOURNEY BEGAN WITH CARVING A SPOON. Many of my students attend the basic spoon carving workshop as an introduction. During this one-day workshop, I always show them my first spoon, which I made more than a decade ago. Although it looks more like a bat, it's a spoon with a handle and bowl. I made a few mistakes, did not know several technical things and did not yet have the required (sharp) tools. **The main goal of my lessons and also in this book, is exactly to avoid those mistakes, skip unnecessary steps in my development and learn faster to ensure that your first creations will be usable, and more beautiful.** Your first spoon will not look like a bat, but like a spoon, although finishing it smoothly may still require some practice. Other spoons like eating spoons, ladles, sauce spoons, feather spoons, dolphin spoons... also require a bit more insight and knowledge. Eating spoons should have the proper width, thickness, shape and smooth finish to ensure a pleasant feeling in the mouth. To achieve this, you need a lot of information and practice. I would like to share the special craft of spoon carving with you. But perhaps this calls for another book, solely about spoons.

This chapter explains the basics of spoon carving by means of a cooking spoon. The purpose of a cooking spoon is to stir in a pan and taste. Therefore, you need a bowl in the spoon. However, size and thickness are less important.

Why wooden spoons? I have been asked this question hundreds of times. My answer, and passion for wooden spoons involves several aspects.

A self-carved wooden spoon is the best spoon ever. It is unique, self-made, from local wood, fits perfectly in your hands and matches your cooking style. Wooden spoons do not get hot, do not scratch, are robust, durable and become even more beautiful with regular use. And they are quiet. Just imagine what meals at primary school would sound like if all children used wooden spoons.

Secondly, the basic and ordinary character of a spoon attracts. A spoon or something to prepare food with is perhaps as old as mankind. As a child, a spoon is probably the first object you learnt to use. We use it every day and you'll find a spoon in every home around the world. It is commonplace and ordinary. **In contrast, there are endless shapes, colours and finishes that make it special.** The perfect spoon does not exist; there is no end, no ultimate goal and it is never finished. Since everyone uses spoons continuously, we all have an opinion about them. Sharing my passion is therefore a special part of the craft. I make most of my spoons in good company, in the woods at the campfire, in the spoon club, at home.... The spoon holds a story and using it invokes memories of the time you made it. A home-made spoon is never just a spoon. **When the spoon is sold or gifted, it's the beginning of the rest of its life.**

At a museum in Sweden, I had the chance to browse the archives in the basement with drawers full of spoons, bowls, jars and dishes hundreds of years old. If those spoons had a voice, they would tell us stories and tales of many people's lives.

THE WOOD

There is no such thing as the perfect wood to make spoons. As illustrated by the picture showing eating spoons of different types of wood, you can make spoons from many types of trees and branches. I prefer dark wood or wood which has heartwood that clearly differs from the sapwood. But sometimes white wood is nice too, when you're decorating or painting. And fungi can turn dull wood into something special. I never use yew for spoons. The wood is poisonous (although you have to eat a lot before it really becomes dangerous) and I'd rather not take the risk. In the end, there are 59,999 other types of wood available.

We always start by splitting through the heart of the trunk or branch, which is why it should be possible to make the desired spoon from no more than half of the branch. **The length of the spoon is the length you have cut.** Make sure there are no cracks in the wood, especially not on the bowl side. If the wood has been drying for some time and you are in doubt, saw off a few centimetres. Sometimes you will notice very fine cracks that may crack further after drying.

FROM BRANCH TO SPOON IN 4 PHASES

Spoon carving, as well as other carving projects, consist of four basic phases that serve as a basic principle: **cleaving, chopping, carving and finishing.** They range **from rough to fine, and from fast to slow.** Cleaving is rough, but is very fast, with one stroke half the wood comes off. The more wood you cleave, the closer you get to the final shape of the spoon, and the less chopping is required in the second phase. A good woodcarving axe allows you to chop to within a few millimetres of the spoon's final dimensions. This is a big surprise for many trainees when they use an axe for the first time. During the second phase, the same rule applies: the more you can chop, the less carving you will need with the

knife in phase three. In the third step, carving involves more control, which is slower than using the axe. The smoother you can finish the spoon with the knife, the less carving or sanding is needed when the spoon is dry. This fourth and final phase is not always required.

I am not promoting speed here, quite the contrary. **Wood or spoon carving is a relaxing activity, which shouldn't involve speed** (unless you want to produce for sale). I'm just trying to provide some efficiency guidelines. For every beginner, it takes quite some time to make a spoon, sometimes a full day. Then, it's nice if you can get the most out of each step in the process. If you get to a result efficiently, it's more fun. This way, you can have a beautiful spoon within hours. **I hope these guidelines will make it easier to find some time in your daily life for**

spoon carving. I learned to master the process of making spoons quickly and needed about 35 minutes to create the spoon in the example. This does not have to be your target, but I like to explain how to use each tool optimally and make you aware of this. **Much more important than speed is fun, peace of mind and joy.**

The four phases I describe here are not universal or all-encompassing. The principles, though, provide certainly enough basics and background to get started, and build upon to **develop your own methodology.** I experiment and apply these principles with some flexibility, depending on the requirements of the wood or shape.

THE AXE WORK IN 5 STEPS

01 **Splitting the wood**

Since we do not use the heart or pith of the wood, we cleave the branch in half. However, the heart is not always nicely in the middle. If you want to keep equal halves (to use both), find the line that goes through the heart as well as through the middle. **Preferably, cleaving results in two equal halves.** The crack applied by the axe usually follows the fibre in a straight line. This also gives you an idea of the direction of the fibres in the wood (which is important when visualizing your spoon). If you want to cleave a small piece of wood off the big block, the crack will most probably slide outwards.

A log splits best when both parts have the same mass and one does not bend more than the other. This way, you can also split alongside the heart, if this makes it easier to obtain two equal halves. But bear in mind that the piece in which the heart remains will have to be cleaved again or will need extra chopping before you can use it. Depending on the size of the wood, you may have to cleave several times to approach the desired

dimensions of the spoon. Or you can reverse it and **match the desired spoon to the dimensions of the wood.**

After cleaving, the heart is at the edge of the piece of wood. In the next step, the heart will be removed to create a usable billet. **The width of the billet is usually determined by the width of the bowl.** The thickness of the billet depends on the depth of the bowl combined with the curvature of the spoon (in the side profile). For this cooking spoon, you need a piece of wood at

least 9¾in (25cm) long, 2⅜in (6cm) wide and 1⅝in (4cm) thick.

For example, if you divide a block into four or eight pieces, like a pie, you might not have enough width for the bowl over the entire thickness, but if we think ahead a bit, later the bowl will be at the bottom of the side profile, which means that the piece of wood only needs to be wide enough there. In the nice piece of ash wood I am using, the top of my spoon will be the round thinner part with the bark. The other flat side is wider, which is perfect for the bowl of my spoon. My billet is still a bit too thick and wide, but cleaving off those few millimetres makes no sense as the split won't continue straight to the bottom anyway and can be chopped off faster with the axe. I could cleave the other half in half, for example, to carve a narrow coffee spoon from each piece.

02 Shaping the back

Before we chop any wood off of the back of the billet, we need to **determine the position of the 'kink' or crank of the spoon.** Looking from the side, the end of the handle is at the very top of the piece of wood, and the handle descends towards the bowl. Somewhere in the bowl, the spoon rises again, like a shovel. **This curve in the spoon does not only make it more beautiful, but also, and more importantly, more useful.** A straight spoon is less handy while cooking, and often machine-made. **That crank is at its best between the middle of the bowl and the back of the bowl** (where the handle starts). Play with those different zones and observe how a spoon looks and works differently.

To shape and chop the back of the spoon blank, you need to determine in advance the position of the crank, and where the front of your bowl and the back of your handle will be. **Use the axe to chop from the mark where the crank comes 'down' towards the front of the bowl first, and then away from the mark towards the end of the handle.** Make sure the back of the bowl is not chopped concave, but rather straight or even slightly convex, like most spoons. It helps to visually mark the front and back of your spoon so you know where to chop. The end of the handle can be at the very top of the billet. The front of the bowl is best not too high because otherwise you will go up too steeply and the fibres will become too short and the spoon will become brittle.

03 Shaping the front

The idea is to create the same shape on the front as you made on the back. You need to decide about the depth of the bowl. Draw the side profile of your spoon, from the handle at the back to the crank, then up again for a bit to the front of the bowl. **The deeper the crank, the more curved the spoon will be, but the less depth the bowl will have.** Find the balance you like. First, chop from top to bottom, towards the bowl; except for the upper part, which I chop in the other direction because of safety (not chopping near the wood hand). Then, you can chop the remaining part, down to the top surface of the bowl.

If you chop in further to shape the crank, you will notice that there is a risk of chopping off the part where the crank rises again. To avoid this, **saw the fibres at the position of the crank.** This is a safety measure to make sure while chopping, cracks stop there and do not continue. As you approach the line, chop more carefully. If you hit too hard, the axe will go straight anyway and you will lose the part of the bowl that goes up again. Finally, chop from the front down to the saw cut. It is difficult to do this safely, which is why you have to put the blank on its side to remove this part.

Grasp the handle underhand with your wood hand and put the bowl end of the spoon blank on the edge of the chopping block, with the saw cut and the part to be chopped facing outwards (i.e. not towards your wood arm). The reason why you should put the bowl around the edge of your chopping block is because it allows you to reach everything with the tip of your axe's blade. If you were to put the spoon in the middle of your block, the bottom or heel of your edge already hits the chopping block before you can chop the furthest corner.

Tilt the spoon slightly and chop gradually from the outside inwards. Don't chop on top of the side of the spoon, because there is too much risk of damaging the bowl. You will find that it's easier to do the bottom part than the top. Therefore, bend your knees a little and chop sideways to remove that last bit.

This is perhaps the hardest part with the axe, but once you master this part, the variety of curves you can apply to a spoon are unlimited.

Now, review and check your side profile and chop away some more where needed. Make sure that the rim at the front of the bowl is not too thick. If it is still ⅜in (1cm), for example, it means you won't be able to scoop out the bottom centimetre of your pan; so ⁵/₃₂–³/₁₆in (4–5mm) is better. Later, use the knife to make it a little thinner.

04 Draw top profile and carve a 'mummy' shape

First, I axe the side profile, then the top profile. This way, the drawing of your spoon remains visible until you start using the knife. If you do it the other way around, you chop away the drawing on the front of your blank when shaping the side profile.

If you want a symmetrical spoon, draw a centreline. Asymmetry is also possible of course, nicely skewed is beautiful, too. Often it's a thin line between skewed and wrong, organic and beautiful. Try to draw the centreline along the direction of the wood fibres. With a ruler, make a few marks at equal distances from the centreline. Connect the dots to visualize the spoon you had in mind. I like spoons with a thin neck. Beginners often opt for a straight handle, but don't always realize that this is much more difficult. **In the case of a straight handle, you don't know in which direction to cut.** If the fibres are slightly wavy, you have to change the cutting direction multiple times along the entire length of the handle. This makes it harder to finish than a handle that narrows or widens.

A handle that gets thinner towards the neck implies you have to be careful when chopping later. Due to the cutting direction, you're going to chop the handle towards the bowl, with the risk of a crack that splits the bowl in half. To avoid this, **we will chop the top profile in two steps.**

The first step starts by drawing a 'mummy'. Draw a line from the widest point of the bowl to the widest point of the handle. Continue this line backwards and around the bowl. Anything outside this **'mummy shape'** can be chopped away (from wide to narrow) without risk of damaging the bowl. This way, difficult areas on both sides of the neck become smaller. First, chop away the parts at the bowl end. Then flip

the blank over, to hold it safely, and chop waste away from the sides of the handle.

In step two, chop away the rest up to the contour of your spoon. To avoid damaging the bowl, **make a saw cut at the narrowest point of the handle left and right,** up to the line of the handle. While chopping down along the handle towards the bowl, any crack created will discontinue at the saw cut. Despite this safety measure, you can still chop too hard causing cracks beyond the cut. Chop carefully and, for sufficient control, keep

your axe arm close to your body. Make sure that the axe cannot go beyond the cut. Finally, chop from the bowl towards the neck.

If this requires slanting your spoon too much to keep it stable during chopping, it is better to put it on the side of the chopping block. This will provide support underneath the spot where you are chopping. Make sure your wood hand is out-of-range and rests on the chopping block. Chop directly towards the line of your spoon, not incrementally inwards. If not, there is a risk of

chopping into the handle every time. By directly following the line of your spoon, the remaining wood will pop off anyway because there the fibres are short.

Since the top profile requires sawing and careful chopping twice, while the side profile only once, this is another reason to take care of the side profile first. This way, the spoon is already thinner when you have to remove the difficult parts to the left and right of the neck. If you don't have a saw, you can use the axe to make a V-shape, but that requires a lot of axe control.

05 Assessment and bevelling the back of the bowl
If all went well, you now have a nice cut-out spoon-like shape or spoon blank, though it may still not quite be what you expected when you drew it or you may have chopped a little too far here and there. **Assess your shape and chop a little more where needed.** If you can, better chop some more off the back than at the front, so your drawing remains.

So far, we have kept the four sides (front, back, left, right) at right angles to each other, not yet rounded. There are two reasons for this. Once you start rounding off, it gets harder to recognize the pure shape of the main sides. In addition, rounding is only one of many ways to make the sides blend into each other. **The exception is the back of your bowl,** especially for larger spoons. Since the axe is faster, I am going to chop off the corners on the back as well.

If you have gone too far with your axe in certain places, it can make sense to make a new drawing of your spoon on the wood. This will ensure carving with the knife is more effective and therefore easier. If necessary, you can first even up the top surface or 'straighten' the asymmetrical parts and then draw.

THE KNIFE WORK

Using the knife grips from chapter 3 you can finish the entire spoon. We hollow out the bowl later with the spoon knife. The following illustrations and pictures show how the grips are applied to the spoon. Finishing a spoon smoothly requires practice and a lot of switching between the different knife grips. Learning where and when to use a grip is a very conscious process at the beginning. I promise you that after a few dozen spoons, it will be much easier, but above all more automatic. This is how you get into a flow, and then it really becomes fun!

Despite the technique and application of the grips, there are still a few difficulties in the process. The following tips and practice will teach you how to master them.

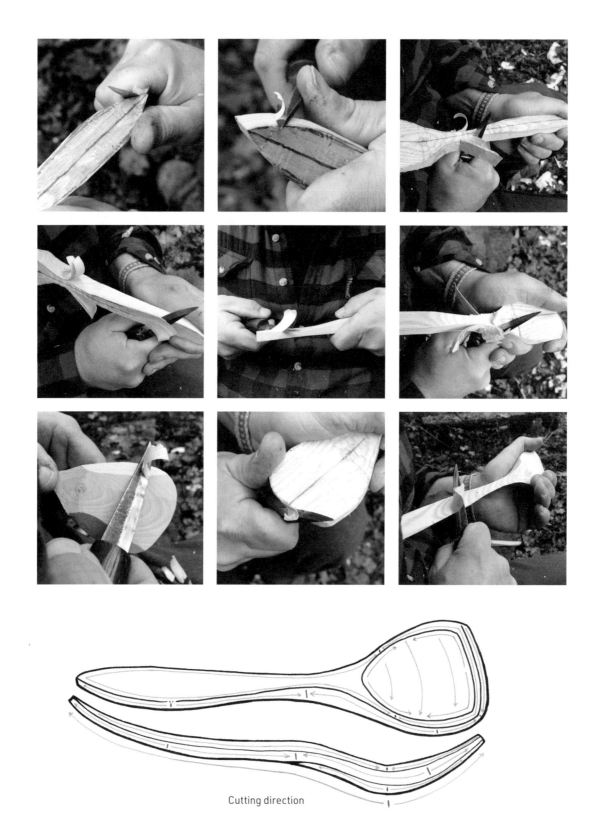

Cutting direction

ORDER OF CARVING

Novice spoon carvers tend to be 'all over the place'. Their eye catches a part that is not right and they carve there, and right after, they start to carve somewhere else entirely. **It makes sense to work in a certain order.** The first thing I do is **address** certain **problems, mistakes or difficulties.** For example, if there is a knot in your handle, cut it nice and smooth first, because sometimes it's a bit more difficult and your handle may be thinner at the top than you thought. In such cases, you will be glad you didn't start at the bottom. If you have a crack somewhere, cut it away first or solve it differently. There is no point in ignoring these problems, as they can make your spoon look very different from what was planned. If you were to finish the handle first and after that you have to reduce the size of the bowl because of a crack, you will suddenly realize that your handle is way too big and you have to start all over again.

Eventually, I am going to **carve the spoon shape twice.** The first time I will shape the main surfaces and carve out the bowl roughly. The second time I will do the finishing and cut facets. **Each time, I begin carving the handle, then the neck and finally the bowl.** At the beginning, it's not always easy to know, remember or feel which grip you should use. With the handle, cut the surfaces with the chest grip and the end of the bottom with the chest-lever grip. This makes it clear and logical. Only after the handle is finished, you can decide how the neck or the transition to the bowl should be like. And only when this transition is done, you can decide how it will transition into the bowl and continue. By focusing on one part, you learn how the fibres run in that area of your spoon and where the cutting direction changes.

THE NECK, A TRICKY AREA

A tricky area to cut nicely or smoothly is the narrowest point of the neck. If the transition has an angle, it's not a problem. **If the transition is rounded or sloping, it can be challenging.** As you always cut from wide to narrow, this area is the transition between two cutting directions. You approach the neck both from the handle and the bowl towards the neck. In doing so, you often cut a little too far against the fibres on the other side. You flip the spoon to remove that little mistake and you're too far again. Sometimes it results in frustration or a neck that is too thin and still not smooth.

You can avoid this by **respecting the order of carving.** If you do the handle first, ignore the curls of wood or slices hanging or sitting on the neck. Don't cut that away every time, otherwise the neck will get thinner and thinner. When the handle is done, carve away the largest fibres from the bowl towards the neck, and shape this area.

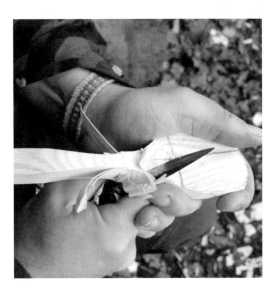

After the handle and bowl, you are going to **clean up the neck.** Tip: use a very sharp knife here, use the chest grip and try to make a long slicing movement from the bowl to the neck as much as possible. This way, you can even cut against the fibres in the neck. You only need to get a few millimetres or ⅜in (1cm) past the deepest point. When the knife finally gets stuck, turn the spoon over and use the chest or thumb grip to cut from the handle to make the transition. Make sure you don't cut into the deepest point again, as it was smoothed out just before.

This is one of the reasons why we keep the spoon 'square-shaped' until the end. Having two flat surfaces meet at the narrowest point of the neck is already not easy; if you were to round it before finishing the neck, two rounded surfaces would have to meet perfectly – which is even harder.

If what's described above still fails, you can lengthen the deepest or narrowest point of the neck as shown on the drawing below. This way, the transition becomes less steep, making it easier to cut a little against the grain.

Extend

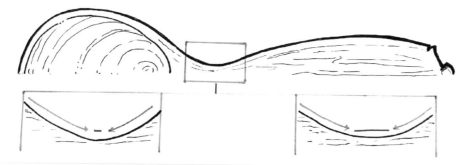

STRONG ENOUGH?

You may have already wondered while designing your spoon or while chopping if the spoon you have in mind will be strong enough. If not, you will definitely have to do so while carving. **The areas where you need to be most careful include the neck of the spoon and the edge at the front of the bowl.** Above all, experience will teach you what is strong enough. Your first handmade spoons will get a nice spot because you are rightly proud. **By actually using your creations, you really learn about the properties of a spoon.** Is it strong and pleasant? Does it have comfortable dimensions for its use? Since they fear a thin, fragile spoon, some keep it very thick. For a laugh at the end of workshops, I often say that we are now going to try to break the spoons. That would be a shame, of course, but you would be amazed how much force you would actually need to break it into two pieces. **There are four elements that affect strength.** Keep them in mind during spoon carving.

01
TYPE OF WOOD

A spoon made of boxwood can be half as thick as a spoon made of willow, and will still be stronger. In fact, the strength of the wood is more decisive than the thickness of the spoon. On the internet and in books, you can find very detailed tables with the different physical properties of each type of wood. If you use wood with spalting, i.e. with beautiful markings caused by fungi, even the strongest wood can quickly become brittle. Therefore, always keep such spoons slightly thicker.

People often think that wood that grows slowly is more compact and therefore stronger. However, this applies to conifers only such as pine, spruce, trees with needles. **With deciduous trees it is exactly the other way round:** these are actually stronger when growing faster. You can clearly see this in the growth rings. For example, I made a spoon from a 1⅛in (3cm) diameter spruce branch with 50 annual rings. The spoon was very thin, yet more than strong enough. If you want to make thin spoons, a hard deciduous tree species that has grown quickly is the best choice. In the Spoonforest, for example, there are a few American oaks *(Quercus rubra)*, which have almost a centimetre gap between two growth rings.

02
THICK AND THIN IN DIFFERENT AREAS

To make an extra thin neck, compensate by making it extra deep in that spot. If the handle is wide towards the end, make it very thin just there. You can use different ways to provide for **strength or sufficient wood in a specific area in different ways.** The simplest shape is uniformly square or round throughout the length of the handle, but by playing with thick and thin, you actually get interesting shapes, like the beech spoon (centre).

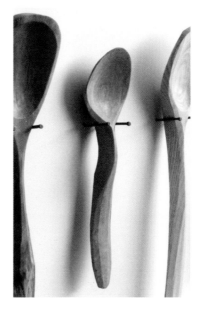

USAGE OF THE SPOON

What will the spoon be used for and how? If you regularly let your food burn in the pan, the front of the spoon will have to be strong enough to resist the wear and tear of scratching it loose. On the other hand, a thin sugar spoon that only serves to make your coffee a little sweeter during your leisurely morning ritual may then be very fragile. You see what I mean. Another great example of this is what I call a mayonnaise spoon: a bowl not too deep (too much mayo is not good for you), but above all a strong neck to be able to knock the remaining mayo back into the jar. Thus, there is something to consider for every kind of spoon. One special place is at the very back of the handle. With many spoons, you never actually hold the back while using it, there is little that can break, so you can make very creative carvings, finials or decorations there.

04

THE LENGTH OF THE WOOD FIBRES

Some types of wood (such as ash and oak) have long fibres, while others (such as beech) have shorter ones. For a long, thin stick of 20in (50cm), the result will be much stronger with ash. For a spoon, however, it is more about how long the fibres of the wood run through the spoon, regardless of the type of wood. We started this chapter with a log with straight fibres. Since we have sloping surfaces in both our side profile and top profile, this means we have shorter fibres in certain places. A straight spoon coming from a straight piece of wood will contain fibres going all the way through the spoon, making it stronger. **If we want a spoon that is super-thin or a shape that is strongly curved (like a ladle), we need to find a branch in which that shape is already present in side profile.** Sometimes a spoon can be made so thin that light can pass through it. That spoon can only be strong enough if the fibre in that part is not interrupted. On the other hand, the edge at the front of the spoon can only be made super thin if the end consists of long fibres that bend all the way through the bowl. With a spoon made of straight wood, this is impossible, because the fibre is interrupted by the hollow of the bowl.

When taking a walk in the forest, I no longer see branches hanging from the trees, but spoons of all shapes and sizes.

SPOON KNIFE AND BOWL CARVING

Hollowing out the bowl is done with a spoon knife. This is a curved wood carving knife that cuts on one side. This means that there is a right- and left-handed model of each spoon knife. Double-sided ones also exist, but I don't recommend them because you often cut yourself and they are also more difficult to sharpen. **Spoon knives come in all sorts of shapes, sizes, prices, steels and with different bevel angles.** Every brand or blacksmith manufactures spoon knives that look slightly different. The price usually reflects the quality, craftsmanship and production time. However, you don't need an expensive spoon knife to make beautiful spoons, nor does **it make sense to buy an expensive knife if you don't have the skills yet to benefit from its full potential.** As your experience grows, you will also be better able to judge which knives and shapes are right for you. On page 128, I make a comparison between some spoon knives to get you started. You can hollow out the bowl in different directions. **I use two steps: rough hollowing and smooth finishing.**

01 **The rough work.** It means removing most of the wood (about 95%) of your bowl without leaving a smooth finish. For this, you use the potato grip and cut at right angles (perpendicular) to the direction of the grain. You start by making a dimple in the middle of the bowl. You make this dimple deeper, wider and larger with each cut. From the very beginning, **you try to carve the bowl shape in a small format, then keep this shape while enlarging it.** Do not carve in depth first, then in width, because it has the risk of cutting deeper again when widening, which might result in cutting through the bowl. **When carving perpendicular to the grain, the advantage is that you can carve the entire bowl in one smooth motion.** If you cut with the grain, you can only cut from top to bottom and not in one go, but that works too. **The hardest part is to find the right starting angle to carve the desired curve.** Beginners tend to put the knife into the wood too steep at first, which quickly gets stuck. First put the knife flat onto the wood (so it doesn't cut yet), then tilt it slightly until you feel the cut just start to 'grab'. That is the correct starting angle.

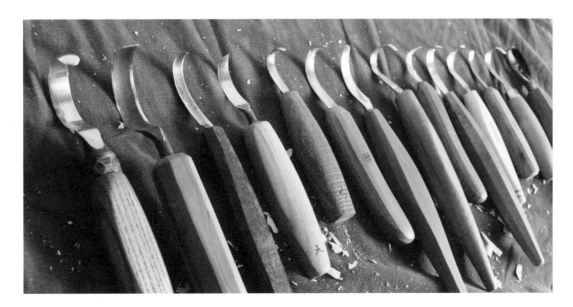

Once you have started, **keep tilting the spoon knife while cutting, so that the blade follows the bowl shape.** You first tilt the knife down, cut a bit, and as you go, start tilting the knife back up, until it comes out again. **Watch out for your thumb!** You can't hide it under the edge with small spoons. Practice makes perfect. As your spoon bowl gets deeper and bigger, hold the spoon knife steeper at the start and you will need to tilt it more and more as it comes back up so the curve or curvature you make with your hand automatically becomes deeper and steeper. To do this properly, the fingers and wrist have to work together to make the right curve. This is where things often go wrong. Then you get a ridge in the middle, because you only cut to the middle and don't tilt enough to get out again. You will feel that sometimes it works well and immediately afterwards it doesn't. This is because **the curve you make with the spoon knife has to be adjusted each time to the** developing spoon bowl (which changes again with each cut).

In the beginning, don't cut away too much at once; keep your focus on the desired curve. When your **spoon knife sounds like peeling a firm apple, you are doing well.** When you hear 'taktak', either the angle is wrong, or the knife is not sharp enough. This is quite tiring and exhausting for fingers and wrist, but it will get better and better with experience. Did you know that this is why spoon carvers can also give good, and especially long, massages? In time, you can squeeze, knead and massage your fingers for an hour on end without feeling pain. Knowing this, a gift voucher for a workshop of spoon carving is the ideal gift for Valentine's Day...in the long run that is. Remember to **feel the edge and bottom regularly** to stop in time, because once you get the hang of it, you wouldn't be the first to end with a hole in the spoon bowl after all. Since the

bowl does not have the same curvature everywhere (often deeper at the back, flatter at the front) and you cut everything with the same knife, it is difficult to get a smooth surface. You can usually clearly see the ripples left by the spoon knife in the bowl.

02 **To finish smoothly** (the remaining 5% of the work), you will **cut in the direction of the fibres. To do this, you need to get the most out of the curvature of the spoon knife.** It helps if the spoon knife has several radii and not just a flat part and half a circle like some cheaper knives. The cutting direction on the inside of your bowl is opposite to that on the outside. So, you cut from the centre line outwards in **four quadrants with their own cutting direction.** The trick is to position the spoon knife in each quadrant so that the curvature fits well with the curvature of the spoon bowl. **The better the curvature matches, the more wood you can cut in one movement and the smoother the result.** On the wide sides of the spoon bowl (where the cutting directions meet), turn the spoon knife up to exit in the middle. Or, at the end, you can cut the fibres at right angles in the middle. You complete the finishing phase using the potato grip, except for the fourth quadrant. There, it gets more complicated. This is where the handle of your spoon gets in the way. I cut this quadrant using **a turning grip.**

Put the spoon bowl in your open hand and hold it between thumb and index finger. Support your spoon knife with the same hand, with the blade in the bowl and the handle just next to or above the handle of your spoon. The remaining three fingers serve as the rotation point on which your spoon knife rotates. Your other hand pushes, along with the three fingers of the holding hand, and cuts by rotating.

Finally, you are going to finish the edge of the bowl. If necessary, you can cut a little more off the outside to get the edge just right, but only a minimal amount, so that the outer shape of the bowl doesn't change too much. I also bevel the top edge at a slight angle; it looks nice and makes the edges less sharp. You can let these edges blend into the handle and turn them into facets or let them disappear altogether.

1   2   1   4   5

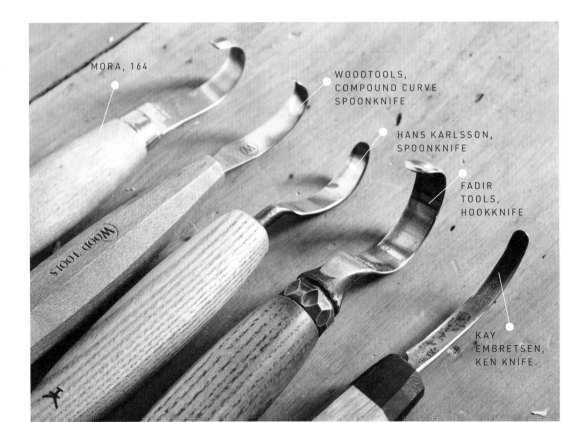

MORA, 164

WOODTOOLS,
COMPOUND CURVE
SPOONKNIFE

HANS KARLSSON,
SPOONKNIFE

FADIR
TOOLS,
HOOKKNIFE

KAY
EMBRETSEN,
KEN KNIFE.

SPOON KNIVES

From left to right (name of maker and name of knife) 1: Mora, 164. 2: Wood Tools, compound curve spoon knife. 3: Hans Karlsson, spoon knife. 4: Fadir Tools, hook knife. 5: Kay Embretsen, Ken knife.

The following features differ between the knives:
Curvature of the spoon knife. The advantage of a particular curvature depends greatly on the bowl shape you want to carve. More curved shapes are ideal for making deeper bowls, while flatter shapes are better for eating spoons. There is not only a difference in curvature between these five knives, but you will also find different curvatures in one knife. Three of the five knives range from (almost) flat to increasingly curved with different radii in between: these are more suitable for precise finishing. The Mora knife, however, starts completely flat and transitions to part of a circle, so consequently has only two variations. The knife by Fadir Tools also has little variation and is perfect to remove a lot of wood quickly.

Shape of the exterior. The exterior can be uniformly spherical or divided into planes. Mora's spoon knife has three surfaces and Wood Tools' knife has two, with a ridge or angle in between. However, the more evenly spherical the back, the easier it slides along the inside of your bowl. The other three knives have this feature, but this requires more effort during the manufacturing process and they are, therefore, more expensive.

Shape on the inside. Kay Embretsen's knife is the only one that has a hollow interior; the others are flat. A hollow interior eases sharpening. Other blacksmiths that manufacture spoon knives with hollow interiors include Belzeboo from Portugal and Lee Stoffer from England – and soon Morini Tools in Belgium!

Handle length. A longer handle is especially useful when using the turning grip (to finish the fourth quadrant), as it allows you to apply more force when rotating on your fingers. This grip also enables you to hollow out bowls quickly and roughly. For large spoons, I often use a 'twca cam' for hollowing out. That is the Welsh name for a large round spoon knife with a thick, 16in (40cm) long handle that is only used in variants of the turning grip.

Steel grade and hardness. It is difficult to judge or describe this property. From experience I can say that the blade of some knives (e.g. Fadir Tools) remains sharp for a longer time than that of cheaper knives.

Angle of the bevels. Like the wood carving knife, the inclusive angle of a spoon knife is 25 degrees. Kay Embretsen's spoon knife deliberately has an angle of 20 degrees, and is therefore not suitable for rougher work. For that, they offer a different, more specific knife. The advantage of such a fine angle is that this knife cuts through the wood smoothly and more precisely, which allows a cleaner finish. Read more about cutting angles in the chapter called 'Swiftly smart sharpening'.

Shape of the handle. Opinions differ on this topic, but I prefer a handle with facets. Facets provide more control when cutting, especially when twisting during hollowing out. A smooth round knife (like Mora's) can move around more in your hand, making it harder to apply extra force with it.

The more you practise and the more experienced you become as a spoon carver, the more you will be able to appreciate the overview above. Yet, there is another way to get a better knife without spending more money. Maybe you are handy with a Dremel and sanding belt to modify the handle and blade of the Mora knife yourself, turning it into a top-notch knife – at no extra cost!

FACETING AND ROUNDING

The final step in carving the spoon is to **connect the main surfaces** (top, bottom and sides); **this is how you turn the spoon into a three-dimensional shape or 'sculpture'.** Sharp edges (at the spoon bowl or handle) can feel uncomfortable in your hand or mouth. There are many ways to carve facets (or bevels) which greatly affect the look and feel. This can make your spoon feel softer or make it look thinner in certain places than it really is. Our eyes mainly focus on the borders of the surfaces and not the surfaces themselves.

Cutting **nice uniform facets** is more difficult than the main surfaces. That's why I think it makes sense to do this at the end. If you had to redo a top or side surface after this last step, the width of the facets is also affected, and then you have to start all over again.

If you prefer to **round the edges,** you can do so step by step by cutting intermediate surfaces first. First, you cut off one corner, creating two new corners, which you cut again, but less deeply. This way, you get a polygon that feels round fairly quickly and is even along its entire length.

RADIAL AND TANGENTIAL

We use these two difficult words to indicate how we get the spoon out of the wood. You can play with the colours of the wood or use the annual rings to have nice little circles in the spoon bowl. Radial means that we take the spoon out of the wood at right angles to the annual rings. This ensures that the two colours of the sapwood and heartwood are visible on the spoon, but also that the annual rings stand out as straight lines on the top surface.

It is totally different when you take the spoon out of the wood tangentially. Then, the spoon lies in the same surface as the annual rings. If you use the bark side or outside of the wood as the top surface of the spoon, annual rings will appear as nice circles in the spoon bowl – with a bit of luck, the sapwood in your handle and heartwood in your bowl. If the bark side is at the bottom of your spoon (what I call 'reverse tangential'), you obtain mostly a cross shape in the spoon bowl and a different balance between heartwood and sapwood.

These choices are only possible if there is colour variation or clearly visible annual rings. For the strength of the spoon, it does not make much difference. Moreover, there are many alternative ways, e.g. removing the spoon from the wood more obliquely. Experiment, try to let the wood surprise you. Together with experience, your knowledge will grow to get the most beautiful spoon from a piece of wood.

If you are totally hooked by spoon carving, be sure to pay a visit to the Spoon Club or the Flemish Spoon Festival! (More info in the chapter 'Wood carving is good for us'.) You can find more details about the finishing, maintenance and protection of handmade spoons in the chapter 'The final touch'. Now, I hope you will actually use the spoon or make someone else happy with it.

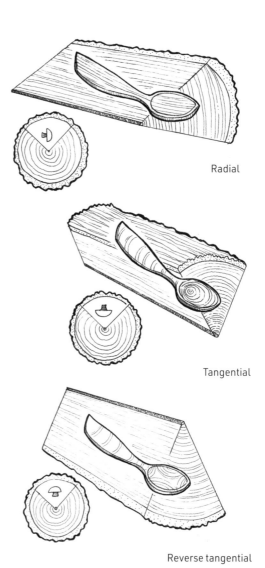

Radial

Tangential

Reverse tangential

06

THE COSINESS OF A KUKSA

THE COSINESS OF A KUKSA

Your handmade wooden mug

APART FROM SPOONS – MY FIRST LOVE – THERE IS ONE ITEM THAT I LIKE TO MAKE PERHAPS EVEN MORE THAN ANYTHING ELSE. It makes me very happy to give it as a gift that is always gratefully received: a kuksa! From the first coffee in the morning to the last dessert in the evening: everything fits into a kuksa. It is much more fun and especially cosier to drink or eat from your own handmade wooden kuksa!

A kuksa, guksi or kåsa is a traditional Scandinavian mug. The Sami in particular make beautiful ones, often decorated with reindeer antlers and delicate decorations. A kuksa is less easy to make than a spoon. On the one hand, it has to be functional in size and shape, just like an eating spoon. On the other hand, hollowing it out is a real challenge (much like a deep bowl) and the process requires attention and knowledge to avoid cracks.

THE WOOD

• **The bigger the diameter of the trunk, the better.** Here, the annual rings are flatter in a kuksa, which reduces the tension when drying and, hence, reduces the risk of cracks afterwards. So, it is recommended to use a trunk with a diameter of 14in (35cm) from which you can carve four kuksas rather than a 7in (18cm) trunk from which you can carve two. As for length, 8in (20cm) is usually sufficient.

• **Soft woods** such as willow, poplar or horse chestnut carve easily, but lack strength. Therefore, the sides should remain thicker, which may give the kuksa a heavy look. Oak and other **harder woods** on the other hand, are tougher for your hands and tools. Moreover, oak, which is ring-porous with large spring vessels, is vulnerable to leaking and is also more difficult to clean. My **favourite woods are somewhere in between.** Alder and maple are fairly soft when fresh, yet strong and less prone to cracking. Beech, in turn, is crack sensitive and less suitable, though could be used. Birch or walnut are good. I prefer to work with cherry or bird cherry (see the kuksa in this chapter) because of the colours, but these types are a bit harder. Special kuksas can be made from burls on trees. The fibres then run in natural tangled patterns and can be fantastically beautiful. Unfortunately, these growths do have a higher risk of holes and cracks. Use what you have, learn and let the wood surprise you!

FROM TRUNK TO KUKSA IN 7 STEPS

01 Splitting the wood

The first question to ask yourself is **what dimensions** you want for the kuksa. The closer you get to the desired dimensions while cleaving, the less axe work is required afterwards. The sample kuksa is 7in (18cm) long, 3½in (9cm) high and has a diameter of 4¼in (11cm). These are average dimensions, but smaller or bigger is of course possible. Compared to an ordinary cup (made of ceramic), a kuksa tends to be bigger or wider, but less deep. Since cleaving is less predictable, it's best to keep some extra margin, but not too much, keeping the axe work in mind. If you can cleave a block about 4in (10cm) high and 4¾in (12cm) wide, you did a good job.

Cleaving a log is most predictable if the mass of wood is split into two equal parts. To cleave a large log, I prefer using a froe because it allows you to make a long straight split. With just an axe, you can't predict how the crack will continue in the rest of the wood. **A froe is handy, but you can also use two axes side by side as an alternative.**

If you want to split a log into three equal parts, you can even do it with three axes at the same time. Then, hit each axe in turn.

I split the trunk into four parts. For the remaining piece, I cleave off the pointed part at the bottom. There is a chance that this may not split straight; in that case, you can chop off the rest. **Stay away from the heart of the wood, preferably at least ¾in (2cm).** This greatly reduces the risk of cracking later. For the same reason, I usually use the bark side as the top of the kuksa, which

brings the thin edges – where cracks are possible – furthest away from the heart of the wood. This position (tangential) also results in nice rings on the inside of the kuksa.

02 **Flattening the top and bottom**
Make the underside flat so you can easily draw on it, the log is stable and there are obviously no cracks. It's not nice if you work the underside at the last minute and only then notice a crack. If you have to fix the crack later, you may get dangerously close to the point where you accidentally make a hole in the bottom of the kuksa.

Also try to shape and finish the top side at this point. It makes drawing easier. If you have to adjust the top edge later, the shape of the kuksa may change too, making it hard to shape a nice circle again. Later, there will be no more wood in the middle to insert the tip of your compass. Actually, **at this point you preferably finish the top surface of the bowl.** You can do the handle later.

You can keep the natural curvature of the wood and make it symmetrical if necessary. This will give your final kuksa **a nice sloping shape with the sides a bit lower.** However, if you opt for maximum volume, it is **better to make the top surface completely flat.**

There remains the question how high you want the handle to be in relation to the bowl. I like it when the handle goes up a bit. That implies that the area of the bowl should be lower overall.

Use the axe for the rough work. After that, it's easier to flatten both surfaces with a drawknife and a spoke shave than using a wood carving knife. This works best if you clamp the block in a vice or shaving horse, or secure it with a clamp to a table.

The drawknife is wider than the kuksa. The blade of a knife is not, so the handle will get in the way. With just a knife, you would have to cut from both sides to flatten the top and bottom surface. A spoke shave works on top of the surface, so width or length don't matter.

③ Designing and drawing

At this point, **you draw the top view of the kuksa on the log.** Basically, a kuksa is a bowl with a handle, but the design variations are unlimited. I like to keep it basic, but some designs also have practical advantages.

Draw the centre line first. If the log still has its naturally curved top, the centre line should be at the highest point along its entire length. The centre line will tell you where to put the compass later and helps to draw the handle symmetrically because you can compare both halves.

The inner circle indicates the size of the hole at the top edge. **The outer circle** shows where to chop and indicates the shape of the bowl. Normal bowls have straight sides from the top down to the bottom, but a kuksa can have a somewhat spherical bowl. Then the walls first run a bit wider from the top towards the outside before coming back in (see the black line on the drawing). This way you can create extra volume with the same diameter at the top. The final thickness of the walls will be $5/32-3/16$in (4–5mm). If you want more bulge in the bowl, make the outer circle $3/8$in (1cm) bigger.

137

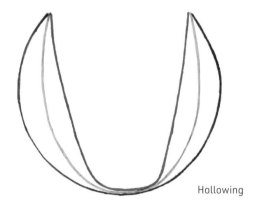
Hollowing

After drying, the kuksa will eventually be slightly oval in the longitudinal direction of the wood. If you want to end up with a nice round kuksa, make the sides of the inner circle a few millimetres wider.

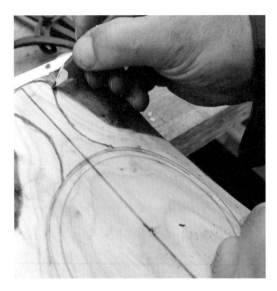

The handle can have many shapes. **The transition from the handle to the bowl is most important. It is better to avoid having an angle here,** otherwise you create an area where the continuous fibres abruptly blend into short quick-drying fibres. By making a curved transition, you reduce the risk of later cracking. If you really want a right angle, carve it after the kuksa has dried. If you are satisfied with your drawing, then step by step you will free the kuksa from the log.

04 Clamping of the wood

You might have expected that we would chop the outside before clamping and hollowing out. Is it better to **carve the inside or the outside first? Both have (dis)advantages.** If you shape the outside first, you can use the axe to go all the way without risk of cracking the bowl. If you do the inside first, the workpiece is heavier and bigger, which is easier to clamp in the first place. However, you have to be more careful with the axe later. A second reason to begin with the bowl is that, with less experience, you don't really know in advance where you are going to end up. By this I mean that when smoothing and evenly carving the bowl, you sometimes go deeper or

wider than your original plan. Thirdly, you can go further with the gouge when the edges of your kuksa are still thick and strong. On the one hand, to obtain a convex bowl, you are first going to cut outwards with the gouge and thus 'undercut' part of it. If your bowl is already shaped on the outside, you cannot use a hammer to do that, because you might hit the gouge through the wood, especially at the front of your kuksa. And on the other hand, when you later use the gouge to carve manually, you can use the strong edge as a lever.

Clamp the log first before you start hollowing out. This way, you can use both hands. The best way (or the most practical solution) is something like a chopping block or stump from which you removed a part or in which you can put pegs. In between, you can clamp the block with packing boards and wooden wedges. You can also use a vice, but the powerful knocks with hammer and gouge are not good for it. A clamp is also possible, but then you need to make the block longer so that the clamps don't get in the way while hollowing it out.

TIP: To avoid cracks, give the kuksa little chance to dry out during the making process. Do not work under direct, hot sun. When taking a break, put the kuksa in water or a damp cloth for a while. For a longer period, you can store it in a sealed plastic bag in the fridge. Ideally, you should completely finish the kuksa in one go, but of course you will only succeed after some practice and experience.

05 **Hollowing out the wood**

Hollowing out a kuksa using only a spoon knife is quite a challenge and causes many beginners to stick to that one kuksa. Too bad! **Hollowing out is much easier by hitting a (curved) gouge** (curvature 7–8 and width of 1–1⅛in/25-30mm is perfect) with a wooden mallet. The first number in the identification of gouges represents the curvature of the cut: 8 is curvier than 5. For a kuksa, you need at least a 7. A 5 is straighter than the curvature of your kuksa. The 'L' represents the curved shape of the gouge. A straight gouge allows you to remove most of the wood and transfers the power of the mallet more efficiently into the wood. A curved gouge allows you to hollow out a little deeper. The last number represents the width of the edge in millimetres. What works best depends on how hard you can hit with the hammer. I like to use a 1⅜in (35mm) gouge, but that may be too wide for others. Also, make sure your hammer doesn't feel heavy and that you can keep hitting for quite a while. A round hammer works better because you don't have to watch which part of the hammer you are hitting with, but a hammer with two flat sides is also fine.

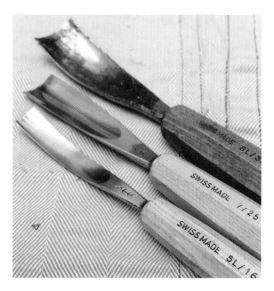

THE BASICS OF HOLLOWING OUT:

I. Always begin at the edge and work towards the middle. Hit the gouge several times while tilting it towards the middle. The deeper you get, the more you have to tilt the gouge between the first stroke at the edge and the last one in the middle. The bowl gets deeper and deeper but remains curved. If you cannot get to the middle using the gouge, you are carving too steeply or too deep into the wood, which will result in an angular bottom that is much harder to smooth out later.

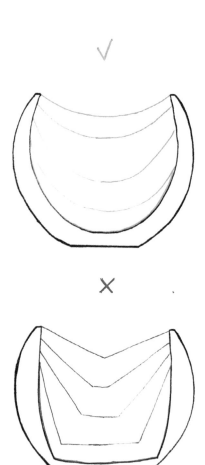

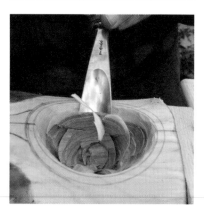

II. If you try to carve out too much wood at once, the corners of the gouge might also cut into the wood, and cause a crack to start from those places. You want to avoid this, especially when working at the side of the bowl. Such cracks can quickly continue through the edge of your bowl. **So it's best to start hollowing out at the front and the back, then progress towards the sides step by step.** As a result, the last two pieces you hollow out are on the sides, but the wood next to it is already removed. This way, the corners of the gouge have less chance of cutting into the wood. In the photo, I have highlighted the crack with a black line to make it visible.

III. That way, you make each part of the bowl deeper. After the sides, start another 'round'. Try to start close to the line, but not so close that you have to keep aiming to position the gouge and progress slowly. **Keep a margin of about ⁵/₆₄in (2mm), which you will cut away later when finishing the bowl.**

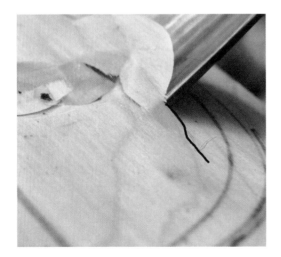

IV. Sometimes feeling is better than watching. Regularly use your fingers to feel how deep or wide the bowl is and whether the inside edges are even and don't have thick parts or gaps. When you have almost reached the desired depth, **use a ruler to check how much you have left.** First check the depth inside the bowl by looking at the ruler alongside the edge. Next, put the ruler on the outside, with the edge sitting at the same height on the ruler. This way, you can see how much you have left at the bottom.

V. If you have the desired shape, it is time to finish it **smoothly.** You continue **using the gouge, but now push it instead of hitting** with the hammer. This way, you can carve thin curls and you won't have gaps caused by hitting it with the hammer. With your left hand (if you are right-handed) hold the gouge by the metal part, just above the edge, and with your right hand push at the top of the gouge. To apply more power, you can use your full upper body to help push, while locking your right hand against your chest. This puts a lot of pressure on the edge of the kuksa. If you carved out the outside first, it would no longer be strong enough. In this way, try to get the bowl as smooth as possible.

To finish the edges very smoothly, you can use several tools. I have all of them (because it's my job), but maybe you don't. Some of these are shown in the pictures. There are two twca cams, which are large spoon knives (one is left-handed and the other right-handed). Similar to finishing the spoon bowl, you need to cut with the grain here. So for a kuksa, it's handy to have both. A spoon knife with a longer handle can also be used, but is not always convenient because the handle gets in the way. The other is a fully rounded spoon knife that has a left and right blade combined in one tool. These three knives are especially useful when you do the outside of your kuksa first and, therefore, cannot apply as much power with the gouge.

However, I prefer the dog-leg gouges; if you can finish smoothly with your gouge, this is the only tool you need. Due to its shape, the dog-leg gouge is great for carving the lower half and bottom of your kuksa smoothly. You systematically cut towards the middle like using a regular gouge. The **shape of the dog-leg gouge allows you to get to the bottom without any problems.** It is also long enough to finish the top half of the edges with the grain. It is difficult to describe exactly how to use this tool. Most trainees consider it a very nice tool that is intuitive and relatively easy to use.

06 Carving the outside

To finish the outside, you will **chop as much as possible using the axe.** That way, you limit the work with the carving knife and other fine tools. In fact, that is hard work, because a kuksa has a lot of end grain at the front and back which is harder to cut than along the fibres. This is a big difference from carving spoons. Therefore, it is important to follow a number of steps to avoid the risk of cracking from the impact of the axe, while still using it as much as possible.

First, you chop the side and bottom of the kuksa, working towards **the front.** All of the strokes are in the same direction. While chopping, the kuksa rests somewhere with its front on the chopping block. In the beginning, this will be on the corner of the still thick block; but as you continue chopping, the supporting point moves more and more forward. These supporting points become increasingly vulnerable as they get thinner. Therefore, make sure you **keep the front of the bowl edge a little thicker and finish this at the end.** It also really helps to make an exaggerated turning slicing movement with the axe; this way you maximize the cutting effect of the axe and minimize the impact on the kuksa.

For **the back half** (the side of the handle), first chop to flatten both sides as curved as possible in the transition to the handle. **I like to make the handle with a hollow at the bottom, close to the bowl;** the part of your hand between thumb and index finger fits nicely into it. You hold a kuksa under the handle, to prevent it from sliding out of your hand, and it should feel comfortable.
To remove the wood under the handle, I use **a**

shortcut, which makes a wood worker's life **much easier.** It's up to you to decide if you do it that way.

First, I drill a hole under the handle, about ⁹⁄₃₂–⁵⁄₁₆in (7–8mm) behind the inside of the bowl. Study the inside of your bowl carefully and try to draw its borders as accurately as possible on the outside. I use the largest drill possible (1¼in/32mm). This ensures that I immediately have a nicely curved shape and makes the next steps easier. Make sure you drill nice and straight and square. **Next, saw from the bottom to the side of the hole.** Try to estimate where the bowl is and keep a margin of about ³⁄₁₆in (5mm). At best, the saw cut ends nicely at the edge of the hole on both sides. Then you can **easily split the wood away in one go** with your **axe.** Pretty exciting, but definitely worth the effort if you want to make some kuksas!

Now, you can chop again as far as possible with the axe. When chopping the back, the kuksa always rests on the handle. The most vulnerable point is the transition between the handle and the bowl. That is where it can break! **Therefore, chop as much as possible at the back of the bowl first, then do the handle.** At this point, also decide what the base of your bowl should look like. It doesn't always have to be round. In fact, if you have a long or heavy handle, it's better to move the base backwards to ensure that your kuksa does not fall over due to the weight of the handle. This implies the base doesn't have to be exactly below the deepest part of your bowl.

First, chop the handle as much as possible like the spoon handle, towards the back. If your handle also has a narrow part, you will have to create a saw cut in these places, and then chop towards the bowl. Unlike the spoon, you do it in two steps. **First saw and chop one side, then saw the other side and chop, but be even more careful.**

Did everything work out fine so far? Good, then the hardest part is over. In the next steps, we're going to use finer tools. It's faster if you use a push knife or spoke shave, but if you don't have one (yet), no problem. Not everything in life should always be quick.

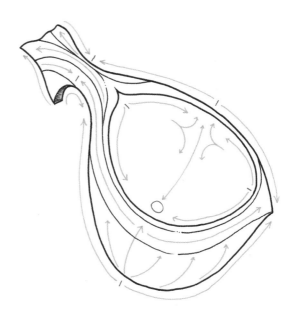

You can use a push knife as a kind of guillotine. To do this, first attach an eye screw in the handle of the push knife. Some push knives already have one when you buy them, but usually they are not strong enough for this work. Also screw an open eye screw into your chopping block. For its position, keep in mind that when cutting with the push knife, your hand does not hit the chopping block, but passes it.

The push knife is the ideal intermediate step between the axe and the knife. A kuksa has much more end grain than a spoon, which makes it harder to cut with a knife. Try to cut as much as possible with the push knife. **The final cuts and smooth finishing can be done with the carving knife.**

Find a comfortable chair, sharpen your knife and practise the knife grips until you are satisfied with the kuksa. You can see the knife grips and cutting directions in the drawing and photos.

A few more finishing tips

• **Preferably do not make the sides of the bowl too thick, and especially make sure they have an equal thickness.** This will allow all parts to dry equally and even deform a little during the drying process, as it needs to bend, or crack. The maximum thickness is about ³/₁₆in (5mm), although that also depends on the strength of the wood. The bottom can be thicker and the edge at the top a bit thinner, of course.

• Pay attention to the top rim and especially that part where your lips touch the bowl to drink. **The rim should not feel sharp, but should also not be too wide.** Otherwise, drops will be left behind, which can then run off on the outside.

• Pay attention to the balance of the kuksa: **does it stand or fall over?** During the axe work, I already mentioned that the base does not have to be exactly under the bottom of the bowl. You can use the knife to refine the base or cut it in a slightly oval or teardrop shape, towards the back. You don't need to flatten the bottom perfectly yet, as it may bulge a little when drying.

• Hold the kuksa in your hands regularly. Everyone's hands are different. If necessary, make the hole under the handle bigger or deeper, until it feels just right!

07 Drying and the kuksa test

Actually, the kuksa is not finished until it dries without cracks and can handle the shock effect of hot liquids like coffee or tea. It occasionally happens that the kuksa does not survive the test, but the more experience you get at the various stages, the less likely this is going to happen. I don't want to scare you, but after every workshop there are always one or two that crack. Fortunately, it happens to me very rarely anymore. The tips in the above sections are not all strictly necessary to apply, but each in itself reduces the risk of cracking. For example, a kuksa with thick edges can also dry well, but the thinner they are, the better your chances.

A kuksa should not dry too quickly. If some parts dry (hence shrink) faster than others, there will be tension that can result in cracks. This usually happens at the top ends of your bowl, i.e. at the front or back.

The drying process takes about three weeks
In **week 1,** put the kuksa in a sealed or folded plastic bag or bread bag in a cold room. Keep the shape of the bag wider than the kuksa and definitely do not pack the kuksa tightly. In this bag, at first the humidity of the air around the kuksa will quickly increase due to the moisture coming out. This will slow down the drying process. To ensure that the wood doesn't go mouldy and the drying process continues, you should turn the bag inside out every two days or replace the bag.

In **week 2, keep the bag open and** place it in a cold, draught-free room. Preferably inside, but better not in the hallway or in a room with many doors. As the bag is open, the moist air can leave the bag easily but slowly and drying continues.

This drying schedule is not science; it is how I do it. But the principle should be clear: slow down the drying process!

All done? Almost. Very occasionally, it happens that a kuksa cracks upon the first contact with hot water. You can reduce the shock effect by letting the oil harden completely first (see chapter 'The final touch'). The sides become less permeable to water and the heat of the water can spread less quickly. You can also let the kuksa get used to lukewarm water from the tap first, and then fill it with warmer water.

Now it's time for your favourite drink! Cheers.

In **week 3**, you can take the kuksa out of the bag and let it dry in that cold, draught-free room for another week. You can feel it with your hands. If it feels cold, there is still moisture inside and you should continue the drying a bit longer. Once it is completely dry, you can do some final finishing with your knife. The wood is also harder now, which allows you to finish some difficult bits a little more smoothly. If you have a type of wood that darkens or gets dirty when drying, like the sample kuksa, carve it again. In the photo you can see how the sapwood turned browner after drying, and after carving it again the original beautiful yellow colour returned.

07

THE MAGIC OF A SHRINK POT

On almost every pot fits a lid

WHAT IS A SHRINK POT? The name says it all: it is a pot that shrinks, keeping the bottom stuck in place. Pick a fresh log and saw it to the desired size. Then, drill a hole along the length of the log and chisel away the wood up to the edge. You finish it nicely with a wood carving knife. At the bottom, you cut a groove on the inside. It will hold a disc of dry wood that will be cut to fit the size of the log.

As the log is still fresh, it starts to dry and therefore shrink, until the disc is wedged in the slot. As a result, the pot is nicely sealed at the bottom. As a finishing touch, you can paint the pot or use the bark or the colours of the wood creatively. Last comes the custom-made lid, which fits nicely and slightly clamps when closing. I know, it probably sounds a bit easier than it actually is. In every step, we will take a closer look at the tools, technique and common difficulties.

A wooden pot made with lots of love and a little magic!

THE WOOD

The basic technique of a shrink pot is, of course, to shrink the wood. That's why we always use a fresh log or branch. The different characteristics of the wood determine the level of shrinkage and the final result. It can sometimes be difficult to determine why a pot did not shrink enough or too much (which can cause cracks).

> **TIP:** Make several pots from the same branch in order to refine your technique based on the characteristics described below until you finally succeed. And sometimes you can be successful with the first pot.

01 THE TYPE OF WOOD

Some species are prone to cracking after drying (like holly or oak) and I prefer to avoid those. **Soft woods** like willow or poplar are more forgiving when shrinking, but very **hard woods** like robinia or yew can also be used. Though, in that case, the groove's dimensions and uniformity must be very precise. **Species with long fibres, such as ash and chestnut, shrink more slowly** and shrink less than other species, but work perfectly. My favourites include maple: very strong and not too hard to process, shrinks well and is nice to finish with various decorative techniques on the white wood. Birch is beautiful when you leave the bark, and like hazel it shrinks very well. I prefer to use stronger and more compact woods with nice

colours – like American bird cherry. It's harder to process, but (almost) never cracks and shrinks nicely. Again, I would say **use what you have, explore and try.**

02 MOISTURE CONTENT

The moisture content of the wood depends on its freshness and how it was stored, as well as on the species and the season in which it was harvested. In spring, when the sap flow is very active, the wood will contain significantly more water than in winter (when the tree is dormant). You can use a moisture meter to gather information and to predict the shrinkage, but you can also do it like I did: **try, adjust or start over.**

03 THE DIAMETER OF THE LOG

Shrinkage is proportional. That is, the larger the pot, the greater the shrinkage. Therefore, you have to take this into account when you determine the size of the bottom plank and the thickness of the edge. Since shrinkage of a hollow tube is a combination of radial and tangential shrinkage, you may expect an average shrinkage of 5–10%, but more or less can also occur (depending on the variables above).

FROM BRANCH TO POT IN 8 STEPS

 Clamping wood and carving the outside
When drilling, it is important to clamp the log as firmly as possible, especially when using a drilling machine. I will demonstrate the subsequent steps by means of **a rustic birch pot with bark and a more austere American bird cherry pot,** where you can see a clear difference between heartwood and sapwood. I also finish the latter pot with a lid.

If possible, use a log that is a lot longer than the desired length of the pot. This has two advantages: **if you want to keep the bark, you can avoid damaging it by clamping the log onto the part that will be removed later.** Secondly, this is **the perfect moment to smoothly finish the outside of the pot** using a drawknife; for example if you want facets (instead of a rounded exterior) or to disclose the heartwood. Start a few centimetres beyond the intended length of the

pot to obtain deep, even surfaces from bottom to top. You can also remove the bark later or decorate it using the wood carving knife, although a drawknife or spoke shave will do

better. If you don't have a vice, you can use a shave horse or tension clamps to secure the wood to a sturdy table. If necessary, use the axe to cut two parallel planes at the bottom of the log, so that the clamps have more grip and the piece of wood is less likely to loosen when drilling.

Drilling
I use **WoodOwl spiral drill bits** with three cutting edges. An ordinary drill will do, but WoodOwl drills even get through dry oak effortlessly. **The larger the diameter of the drill bit 1 or 1¼in (25 or 32mm), the easier it is to hollow out using a gouge afterwards.** If you use a smaller drill bit, you can drill two or more holes next to each other or overlapping, which will save time when hollowing out. This is especially useful in case of a wide pot, unless you drill with an auger. **An auger** is a long spiral drill with a transverse wooden stick as a handle that you turn manually. Since we are drilling into the transverse wood (perpendicular to the longitudinal direction of the fibres), it is important that the auger is very sharp. Augers can drill through the fibres, but are sometimes not sharp enough to drill through end grain. **Drill straight** to ease the hollowing out later and, in case of a narrow pot, to prevent you from going through the side. It helps if someone checks from the side whether you are drilling straight in the longitudinal axis of the wood; it is difficult to see this yourself. Or you can put a mirror next to you. **After drilling, saw the obsolete wood from the shrink pot.** By drilling, a lot of wood has been removed, which makes the sawing easier.

③ Hollowing out the pot

First hollow out roughly with the gouge. The thickness of the wall depends on the diameter of the pot. Not counting the thickness of the bark, which provides little strength. For narrow pots, my wall is about ³/₁₆in (5mm). Thinner is not possible because we need this thickness to cut the groove. For larger pots (from 4in/10cm), I keep a side of ⁹/₃₂–³/₈in (7–9mm). Only for giant pots (bucket sized) I use ³/₈–¾in (1–2cm). In general, a thin wall allows the wood to shrink more easily. If the wall is too thick, the wood cannot deform easily enough and the risk of cracking increases. This also applies when the wall does not have the same thickness all around. On the other hand, the function of the pot also partly affects the thickness of the walls. If you want a sturdy little pot for coffee that joins you everywhere in your backpack, it is better to have slightly thicker sides.

For hollowing out, **a gouge with inner bevel (incannel) is ideal.** Normally, the slant towards the edge is on the (convex) outside of a gouge. These gouges have the bevel on the inside. As a result, the full length of the convex side is in line with the cut. This is ideal for cutting straight pieces and creating straight sides. Put the chisel in the middle, on the edge of the hole. Then **hit it with the wooden mallet (like the kuksa) and chop to remove wood bit by bit towards the edge.** Try to cut pieces with equal thickness down to the bottom. The maximum thickness is just a little less than the height of the curve of the gouge. Be careful to make sure that **the corners of the bevel do not enter into the wood,** otherwise the gouge is likely to get stuck. Then, you lose time you hoped to gain by cutting large pieces very quickly, because you have to free your gouge every time. If it happens, turn the shrink pot over, hold the gouge and hit the chopping block with the edge of the pot. (Watch out for your hands!) If it doesn't let go, there is no option but to use another gouge or drill to remove the wood from around the gouge to loosen it. Be sure not to pull out the gouge while holding the pot with your other hand. As soon as it loosens, your muscles will react automatically and your hand with the gouge will shoot back to the pot and perhaps into your other hand.

If the fibres go nice and straight through your pot (as in the bird cherry pot), everything can be carved out from one end, but sometimes you have to turn the pot over and **work from the other end as well.** The birch pot had lots of side branches giving the bark a nice look, but because of that the fibres inside are curvier at these thickenings. I had to cut those from both ends, leaving the middle a bit thicker. This results in more work with the knife to smoothen the inside later.

Mark the thickness of the edge using a pencil. By sliding your middle finger along the edge while pressing firmly against your index finger, you can draw a line manually at equal distance from the edge. This takes a little practice, but is handy and easy. If you don't have a gouge with inner bevel, you can hollow out with a wood carving knife or spoon knife.

Then finely hollow out smoothly with the knife. After using the gouge**, switch to a wood carving knife to smoothen the inside.** Some prefer to do this with a spoon knife, which is easier. But you

really get the best result with a straight knife. Technically, this is the most difficult part of making a shrink pot. Hold the pot firmly against your chest with your wood hand and **move (or apply force) with your knife simultaneously in three different directions:**

1: Rotate your wrist counterclockwise following the curvature of the pot. However, if you only make this movement, the blade will not cut, but rather jump forward leaving gaps or ridges in the wood, rather than a smooth surface.

2: At the same time, push the knife down until your hand touches the pot or your wood hand. So, use the full length of your knife to maximize the slicing motion.

3: Constantly push the right side of the blade hard against the side of the pot while moving.

This combined movement takes some practice, but with this you will make the surface you are carving nice and smooth.

Meanwhile, pay constant attention to the position of your wood hand! If the knife is longer than the length of the pot, it may wound your hand at the bottom.

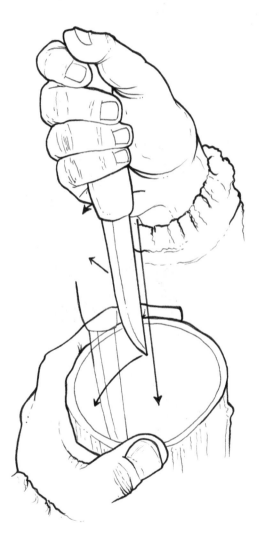

Tips: This movement can cause pain on the side of your carving hand, just below the little finger, as it pushes against the edge of the pot. Therefore, use the index finger of the wood hand as a support cushion by letting it protrude just above the rim.

If the bottom edge has become too thin for the groove you still have to cut, flip your pot and use this end as the top edge. Or saw a part off your pot because typically the edge is thicker a few centimetres down.
If the pot is twice as high as the length of the knife, it is easier to finish the middle piece with the spoon knife or gouge.

04 Cutting the groove

Once the inside is nice and smooth, you can cut the groove. Traditionally, this was done with a wood carving knife, but that is difficult and requires a lot of knife control. There is an easier way, but it requires an extra tool. **Mark where the groove will be**. Do not put it too close to the bottom edge to avoid pieces breaking off. Depending on the size of the pot and the thickness of the bottom, do this in ⁵⁄₁₆–½in (8–12mm) above the bottom edge. Ultimately, you don't want the bottom board to come out under the bottom edge of the pot. If you want legs for your shrink pot, the groove should be higher (see below). You can mark it with a pencil or a **marking gauge** with a blade (not a pin). This way, a small groove is made all around which you can then follow with one 'leg' or the cutting edge of the V-gouge. I prefer to use the KN24 V-gouge by Flexcut. This tool is great for cutting this groove, but I'd prefer the cutting edges to be just a little longer. But then you have to make a gouge yourself. **With the V-gouge you cut a V-shaped groove, always at the same angle and on the line.** You do this twice. The first time you don't go deep, but try to stay controlled on the line. The second time you go as deep as possible (about ⅛in/3mm), until the V-gouge disappears into the wood completely.

05 Make the bottom plate

Unlike the shrink pot itself, the bottom plate or disc must be **completely dry**. There are many different ways and tools to customize the base. It all depends on your experience in wood working, the tools available and what you like. In the most traditional way, you use a piece of wood that you cleaved and dried some time ago. First, you plane or carve this piece with a drawknife to a thickness of ⅛in–³⁄₁₆in (3–5mm) (again, depending on the size and purpose of the pot). Then, you can cut it completely with a wood carving knife or reduce it with a (scroll) saw first.

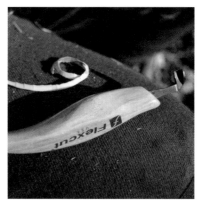

At the other end of the 'tool spectrum', you can use a board from an old wine box. You cut it out with a jigsaw and finish it with a belt sander. My method is something in between.

First, plot the inner contour of the bottom onto the plate by putting the pot onto the wood. Make sure the pencil is thin and sharp and draw diagonally to be as close as possible to the inner **contour** of the pot. Also mark the shrink pot and the plate with a line to remember its position then you won't have to puzzle the disc into the pot afterwards. **Saw and/or cut out the plate,** keeping the pencil line at the outer edge. If everything went well, the plate should fit perfectly, but often you need to trim here and there. 'Fit' means – depending on the type of wood, humidity and also the diameter of the pot – the following: for a small pot with little shrinkage, the bottom should be sized to the

point where you really need to push and click it into the groove. For a large pot with more shrinkage, it's good that the bottom fits in nicely, but just doesn't clip; otherwise the pot cannot shrink enough.

Finally, cut or sand a sharp edge to the bottom plate. After all, the groove you made is V-shaped and the bottom should fit into it. If you used Flexcut's V-gouge, the V is not nicely perpendicular to the lengthwise direction of the pot, but almost completely at an angle. In this case you only need to make a bevel at the bottom of the plate to make it fit. When carving, pay close attention to the direction of the fibres. One incorrect cut (against the grain) can break it. Machine sanding is faster and with some practice produces a nice even result.

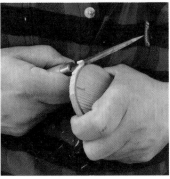

06 Shrinking the pot

You have **two options.** First option: you let **the wood do its thing** and set the pot aside to dry and shrink. This will happen faster in a warm ventilated room than in a cold enclosed space. Depending on various characteristics of the shrink pot and its environment, shrinking may be complete after a few days to weeks. If you want to be completely sure, you can weigh the shrink pot regularly. The pot gets lighter and lighter as the moisture dries out; when the weight remains the same, the pot is dry.

If you can't wait that long**, use the second option with the microwave as your best friend!** I place the shrink pot in the microwave for periods of 1 minute. In between, it has to cool down for a few minutes (you can see the vapour coming out of the pot). As long as the pot doesn't get too hot (so you can't hold it anymore), it's fine. It can be completely dry after 10 to 15 times. If you let it get too hot, cracks may appear. If you want to char wood quickly, you should put it in the microwave for 20 minutes. But then you risk fire and a broken microwave. Don't ask me how I know that.

Shrinkage can make sure the bottom fits very tightly, but **it will never get waterproof this way.** If you still want to use your pot for liquids, you can seal the groove between the wall and the bottom on the inside with beeswax. Unfortunately, it is not compatible with hot liquids, as beeswax melts at about 140°F (60°C). So, for coffee, it is better to make a kuksa.

07 There is a lid for (almost) every pot

I didn't make a lid for the birch shrink pot; it serves perfectly well for pencils, paintbrushes or toothbrushes. It gives an extra touch if you do **not leave the top edge flat but cut it into a (curved) shape.** You can do the rough work with a saw, and finish with the wood carving knife.

For the other pot, I will explain how to make a lid. Since the pot is completely dry, it can be made to measure. There are several ways, as I will show later. **A two-piece lid, with an inner and a top disc, is the easiest. A knob completes the lid, but is not necessary.**

You cannot draw the shape of **the inner lid** exactly as we did with the bottom. Put a sheet of paper on top of the edge of the pot, and press the inner edge of the pot into the paper by scratching it with your fingernail. Then, you can mark the line with a pencil to make it clear. Cut the shape out of the paper and plot the outer edge of the paper onto the plate. Saw and cut out the inner lid as you did with the bottom. Again, I usually use pine, as this is more readily available in planks from wine crates and the like. In order to glue the top lid to the inner lid in the right place later, **I make sure the inner lid fits perfectly into the pot.** By 'perfect', I mean that it fits exactly, but is clamped between the sides at the same time. For the final adjustments, a disc sander comes in handy, but carving will do the trick as well.

I like to make the top lid, which is always visible, from beautiful pieces of wood that I have collected or cleaved and dried myself. This lid comes from an apple tree from which I have cut end grain slices so you can see the annual rings on top. Few types of wood are suitable for this, as especially thin slices crack very easily when drying. Fruit species sometimes work particularly well, as do chestnut, robinia and catalpa. **Make the top lid slightly larger than the pot;** about half a centimetre is what I usually like best. If you were to make the lid exactly the same size as the outer edge of the pot, there is a good chance they won't match nicely when closed.

To glue the two lids together, I spread wood glue on the inner lid. Then, I turn the pot over and put it on (the bottom of) the top lid. As the inner lid clamps nicely, by observing it from the top, you can position the pot very easily. Let the glue dry according to the instructions. Finally, you can pull both lids out of the pot together.

As the inner lid was made to clamp, the lid does not fit nicely on the pot yet. **Carefully carve the inner side of the pot a little bigger until the lid fits easily.** As they fit very tightly, you can turn the lid a little to secure it into the pot and it cannot fall out. To open, turn the lid a little in the opposite direction. If it is difficult to see how the lid fits into the pot, you can cut a small notch in the inner side of the pot, and at the corresponding position on the side of the inner lid. This way, you can quickly find the right position.

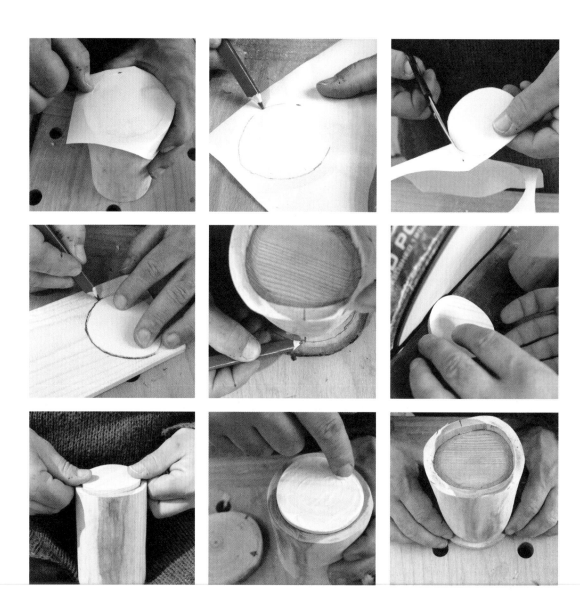

08 Making the knob

The cherry on the shrink pot is the knob. Actually it's totally unnecessary, because if the lid grips by turning, you don't need a knob to open the jar at all. But not everything has to be functional. **Chop and cut a piece of wood into a nice shape.** I used a piece of bog oak here. Drill a hole through the lid where the knob should go and glue it in place. It's as simple as that. With the tips below, making and gluing the knob is easier.

- If you **make the hole conical,** i.e. where the diameter of the hole reduces downwards, you have two advantages. First, it is easier to make the knob fit. This is because you also make the knob conical, and if the lower part is a bit too thin, you just push it a bit deeper until it fits properly. Secondly, this way the knob also makes more contact with the inner wall of the lid, so the gluing will be stronger. You can buy such a conical drill or you can make your own by grinding a metal drill conical. You will have to drill a small hole first with an ordinary wood drill and enlarge it with the conical drill bit.

- Carve the knob **at the end of a longer piece of wood.** This way, you have more grip while carving, and you only saw it off when it's almost finished. For the final finishing, you can also insert the knob into the lid for that very same reason.

- If you want to **oil** the lid, **do it before gluing the knob.** Glue penetrates deeply into wood that has not been oiled. If you only apply the oil afterwards, there will be (glue) spots where the oil does not penetrate. You can see this very well in the end by the colour difference.

- Make sure the knob goes through both lids at the least, so there is as much contact as possible between knob and lid. Afterwards, you can **saw off the knob in line with the bottom** of the inner lid.

09 Making up pot variations

Once you get the hang of it, you can decorate the pots in many different ways (see next chapter). You can also make variations on the type of pots above. There is not enough space here to write them out completely in steps and with pictures, but the explanation below can certainly get you started to make your own unique pots.

Square pots

You can carve the outside of the pot square with your axe and drawknife. However, the inside shall not be completely square. The sides are roughly straight, but rounded at the corners. This way, on the one hand, the bottom will fit better when shrinking, and on the other hand, it's much easier to smoothly finish rounded corners with your wood carving knife than to make straight corners inside your pot.

Pots with feet

If you make the groove further from the bottom edge and shrink the bottom a little higher in the pot, there is room at the bottom to cut away parts of the pot. This will give your pot legs. This is slightly more difficult than an ordinary pot, because the inner side has to be even everywhere; after all, you can only mark the inner side at the bottom with your pencil. It is also less easily accessible using the V-gouge.

OTHER TYPES OF LIDS

One-piece lid

You can also carve the upper and inner lids together from one piece of wood. This is the easiest with a square or rectangular pot because

you only need to saw four sides. Sawing a round shape requires a lot more cuts. First, shape the lid so it is the right size for the upper part above the pot. Then, saw away the parts at the bottom to shape the inner part of the lid. Finish with your wood carving knife. If you feel like carving a lot, you can even make the knob in one piece together with the lid.

Inset lid

This kind of lid works best when the inner side of the pot has an even shape, i.e. round, square or rectangular. Using your marking gauge and your V-gouge, make a groove at the top of your pot about ⅜in (1cm) from the top edge. Then, cut away the wood between the groove and the top edge with your wood carving knife, about ⁵⁄₃₂–³⁄₁₆in (4–5mm) deep. This will result in a flat ridge inside your pot, for which you can create a disc as a lid that fits nicely. In this case, you need a knob to remove the lid from the pot.

Locking lid

There are many different ways to create lids that can really be sealed. One of the most elegant is shown in the picture. The top edge of the pot – except for two opposite protruding parts – is cut and lowered. Then, make a lid exactly the right size to fit the pot, with both protruding parts of the side nicely cut from the lid. The yellow piece of boxwood on top of the lid is loose and is the closing piece. You create it by gluing the knob into the lid and making the hole of the closing piece just a little bigger, so it can still rotate. Make a groove on the inside of the protruding parts of the pot just above the lid. Cut the closing piece to make the ends fit exactly into the grooves. To open the pot, turn the closing piece away from the grooves; to close, turn it back into the grooves.

08

THE FINAL TOUCH

THE FINAL TOUCH

Finishing
and decoration

When you're done carving and the wood is completely dry, there are still various options to finish, treat or decorate your object. For beginners, I will cover the frequently asked questions first: 'Should I sand or not?' And: 'How can I protect my spoon?' Then, I give some tips and tricks on decoration techniques that will get you started. Unfortunately, there is no room to explain more complex techniques such as kolrosing or chip carving. Although I usually prefer to keep the natural colours of wood, there are a few ways to make the woodwork even more beautiful or unique. Whatever you do with your wood carvings, one thing you should definitely *not* do is to put them in the dishwasher! So just do the dishes by hand, cosy together.

TO SAND OR NOT TO SAND, THAT IS THE QUESTION

WHY SHOULD YOU SAND?

First comes the question: **what is smooth enough?** The answer, of course, is subjective. Moreover, there is **value in the visibility and traces of the tools** used to make something. These traces show that the object was handmade and represents the skill and creativity of the maker – totally different from the perfection of a machine. Some of the most beautiful spoons I have seen were not perfectly carved, but rather very special because of their creative shape or wood texture. On the other hand: perhaps there are wood carvers who put too much effort into finishing to compensate for lack of creativity? Let's just not judge too quickly and above all find out what is beautiful, creative and valuable and what was created with heart and soul. Some carvers transform **rough finishing into an art rather than an incompetence.**

First, function determines whether an object is smooth enough. A kuksa does not have to be as smooth at the bottom; after all, your lips never touch it there. At the edges, it should feel pleasantly smooth and ensure no drips are spilled. Of course, if the finish is so rough it becomes difficult to remove food residues after using a kuksa or spoon, I wouldn't consider that smooth enough.

Second, on a convex surface, it is hard to achieve the same smoothness with cutting tools as with sanding. Flat surfaces can be made nice and smooth with planing, while hollow areas can be carved as smooth with a knife. With most convex surfaces, that is almost impossible.

Smooth carving implies that you cut off corners again and again until the entire surface is smooth enough. Sanding goes a step further and it is therefore quite defensible if you sand these surfaces.

In my opinion, sanding is all too often perceived a bit pompously as a quick fix to compensate for lack of craftsmanship in being able to carve smoothly. It is completely understandable that novice carvers can't yet manage to get a surface as smooth as they would like.

WHY NOT SAND?

First, if you decide to sand, take your time. Start with a coarse grit – 80 or 100 – to get the surface smooth in a reasonable amount of time. The wood will feel smooth, but the scratches of the sandpaper will still be visible. Try to sand with the grain direction as much as possible; these scratches are easier to remove using thinner sandpaper. Next, sand with 150 or 240 and again with 400. Of course, you can also sand finer until your wood shines like a mirror or until you are satisfied. If you were to start sanding directly with 400 grit, you'd be at it for a really long time. If you skip steps, you won't be able to remove the scratches left by the previous grit. Use at least three different grit sizes.

Sanding takes a lot of time. I know good carvers who make a beautiful spoon in one hour and subsequently have to sand for at least another hour until they are satisfied. In the end, you can become a skilled sander, but even then it is time-consuming.

It takes even more time if you know **what happens to sanded wood when it gets wet!** The fibres of the wood that have actually been sanded (and damaged) are all evenly flat, but when they get wet, they swell and straighten up. Then you get that unpleasant feeling like when licking the last bit of an ice lolly off its stick. You can avoid that feeling by wetting your spoon after sanding and sanding away the straightened fibres using fine sandpaper. It's advisable to do that two or three times. As I said, sanding is really a lot of work if you want to do it right.

Second, a spoon or kuksa shape is difficult to sand with tools other than your hands and a sheet of sandpaper. It is usually the thumb doing the hardest work. A thumb is soft. As a result, it is very difficult to keep the edges between two surfaces – and thus the facets – sharp. **You can often recognize a sanded spoon because everything is rounded.** Not a bad thing if you like that, but it does limit your choices. You could experiment by wrapping sandpaper around a small block or dowel to work on faceted areas.

Third, a sanded surface loses its shine much faster after use. Many wooden objects in our homes have been sanded without us knowing. Anyone who has ever seen the shine of a board finished with a very sharp plane will realize that most wooden furniture and boards in our homes are sanded. I love how light reflects on a surface that has been cut with sharp tools.

Fourth, sanding generates dust! This is not an insignificant difference from the shreds and curls of all shapes and sizes you get when carving. Convincing your housemates to carve in the house is one thing; sanding is something else. Dust you need to remove with a vacuum cleaner, it's everywhere, and no, it's not that healthy either.

OIL

Why would we oil our wooden spoons or bowls at all? Or what happens if we don't?

PROTECTION

Wood consists of fibres and vessels made up of cells. Therefore on the surface of your carvings, you have cut cells everywhere, which are actually tiny holes. With oak, you can see the holes in the springwood with the naked eye, but with other species you usually need a magnifying glass. When you oil your carvings, those holes are filled with oil. **If you don't oil a spoon or cutting board, food remains more easily in those holes.** That being said, when it comes to hygiene, it is mainly about washing it properly after use. By cleaning properly and drying well afterwards, harmful bacteria have little chance to multiply. In fact, recent studies show that plastic cutting boards carry more bacteria after washing than wooden boards. On the one hand because wood is a more flexible material that can be cleaned more thoroughly. On the other hand, some types of wood contain antibacterial substances.

A spoon without oil will inevitably discolour quicker due to contact with food. The spoon in this photo is made of light brown cherry wood and has been used by my sister pretty much every day for the past three years. When I gave her the spoon as a gift years ago, it had just received a coat of walnut oil. Frequent washing gradually caused the oil to come off. When I visited her, I could sometimes still see what they had eaten the previous day. Red cabbage or tomato sauce leave their colour even on the best plastic pots. This spoon was always washed well, but still some colour remained. After an accumulation of colours, and also under the influence of sunlight, the wood will get darker and darker. The black spots were caused by letting the spoon burn on the edge of a pan.

What is considered 'dirty' to some is patina to others. It depends entirely on how you look at life. I like a spoon that shows it has had a meaningful life in someone's kitchen. In short, if you want to preserve the colour of the wood for as long as possible, it is a prime reason to use oil.

AESTHETICS

Even for a humble spoon, appearance counts. This is a second reason to oil your work. To me, that is often the most enjoyable moment when an object is finished. 'Finished' then also includes burning or ebonizing (which is described later). The oil brings all the colours in the wood to life.

The shades are warmer and small decorations, annual rings and details in the wood stand out more. The effect is particularly striking in darker types of wood. After a few washes, the warm colours fade and the wood becomes duller again; then it is time for another coat of oil. We have been using the cooking spoon in the photo almost every day in the kitchen for years. The oil intensifies the brown heartwood of the plum wood.

GOOD OIL

A suitable oil has two important characteristics: **it should be edible and it should be a drying oil.** Oils such as tung oil, linseed oil or walnut oil contain a high percentage of unsaturated fatty acids, which allow the oil to dry and harden by the influence of oxygen, light and heat. This chemical process is known as **polymerization**. The unsaturated fatty acids react with the oxygen in the air and create molecular chains, or polymers. The more oxidation, the thicker the oil. Eventually it is completely oxidized, i.e. hardened

or dried into an elastic polymer. This hard layer protects the wood and makes it even less permeable, thus increasingly water-repellent. Other, non-drying oils have proportionally far fewer unsaturated fatty acids and will never dry completely. The best-known example is olive oil, but most oils we use in cooking do not dry or dry extremely slowly. With exposure to air, the oil will quickly turn rancid and remains sticky.

Besides fatty acids, oil also consists of residues of the seed or nut from which it is pressed, antioxidants and proteins. Some oils are refined as much as possible after pressing to remove all the superfluous substances that do not contribute to the drying process or even slow it down, but provide flavour and colour. These oils are made especially for the wood worker, but pricy.

The polymerization process can take up to a month at room temperature with average humidity for tung oil and even longer for other

oils. **Except for kuksas, I rarely wait so long.** This means that the oil layer is dry but not yet fully hardened and will wash out a bit faster, especially when using detergent. But if the wood turns a bit dull, you can simply apply another layer of oil. My favourite is **walnut oil.** I love the smell, it makes the wood a bit darker, but not yellowish like linseed oil. It hardens fairly quickly, but slower than **tung oil.** So why don't I use the latter? My walnut oil comes from a press a few kilometres from our house, while tung nuts (which are actually the seeds of the tung tree, but resemble nuts and thus do not cause an allergic reaction to nuts) grow on the other side of the world. **Grape seed oil** is also a possibility; it is completely colourless, dries more slowly, but can also be a solution for people with nut allergies.

APPLYING THE OIL

Oil is a protective top layer that fills the open pores. Since drying also requires oxygen, **I don't** think it **makes sense to soak your wood in oil for a long time.** After all, it is only the outer layer that eventually dries and hardens. Usually, I use my hands or a cloth to rub the oil into the wood well and abundantly. What wasn't absorbed after half an hour, I wipe off again. If you want to speed up the process, you can put your carvings in the oven. **At a temperature of 122°F (50°C), the polymerization process is accelerated and takes just some hours instead of weeks.** The molecules move faster, thus find other molecules to form polymers together faster. Warmer is also possible, but make sure you are not baking the wood (see below). **Preferably store the oil in a dark place or in a dark bottle,** not too hot, and always keep it closed as much as possible. This slows down oxidation and oil going rancid. Under good conditions, most oils will keep for one to two years.

DECORATIVE FINISHING TECHNIQUES
PAINTING

To me, working with paint does not mean creating works of art, but bringing colour and joy, especially to pale woods. After painting, you can also cut away parts creatively to make the wood visible again in patterns. I like using chalk paint because it has a matt finish. It is available in several beautiful colours and can be kept in jars. Several wood carvers use ecological milk paint, which requires you to mix the paint powder with water. The advantage is that you can combine colours yourself and store it much longer than the jars I buy that end up drying out anyway. If you like painting, it's definitely worth looking it up and trying!

For pots and spoon handles, especially on light woods, paint can be a nice extra. However, I never use it on parts that get into contact with food, such as the bowl of a spoon. No matter how natural or ecological the paint is, most pigments contain substances you don't want in your mouth.

BURNISHING

In Dutch, we call it 'frotting'. It is what you are going to do basically: rub hard with an object on the wood to smoothen it. It's no panacea that clears all the pits and bumps, but in case of smooth-cut objects, it can compress the fibres just that little more, to make the surface feel smoother and shinier. The idea is that you use an object that is harder than the wood you are working with. You can buy porcelain or hard plastic burnishers for this. You can also use horn or smoothed pieces of bone. Personally, I use a few stones that once came home as a souvenir from a trip. Ideally, you should have a few different curves and straighter parts to do good 'frotting' on every surface of your workpiece. Be careful with facets though: if you want to keep them nice and tight, don't rub on the sharp edges, otherwise you will round them and they will be less pronounced.

BURNING

Burning a spoon, coat hook or shrink pot might seem a bit drastic, but with a manual gas burner you can blacken very locally or target specific parts. It's surprising how you can play with the distance between flame and wood. This allows you, for example, to blacken only the edges and leave areas a few millimetres away from the flame untouched. You can also spare deeper-lying areas that you have carved out to make the relief stand out. Or you can work in reverse and, for example, burn a pot and then cut away or partly sand off pieces, to obtain more contrast between the black parts and the parts where the wood becomes visible again. With some practice, you can even play with different shades of black and brown.

Should you burn just a little too long or too close at the same area, the wood can really catch fire. Usually, you can just blow out the flames, but I always do this outside – and within reach of water for extinguishing if necessary – just to be sure; and because of the smoke. After burning, soot will come off the black surface. This black particulate consists of carbon particles and other substances that can be harmful. And you don't want your hands, tools or clothes to turn black. In short: after burning, wash well until no fine black dust comes off anymore.

EBONIZING

Ebonizing is an ancient technique for colouring wood black. **The name comes from the world of furniture restoration, where it was used to mimic the now rare, endangered and very expensive black ebony.** The technique was especially popular in the 19th century. There are other ways, such as ink or stain, to make wood black, but the most natural-looking result is obtained by ebonizing. This technique is based on a chemical process in which iron acetate reacts with the tannins in the wood, which can turn the wood brown to black.

To make iron acetate, you need vinegar, preferably the cleaning variant that contains more acetic acid than the kitchen variant. Pour it into a jar with a lid. Now, you need **iron**. Very fine steel wool works fastest. As these are often coated with oil against rusting, it's best to clean it with some detergent and then let them dry well. Next, put the ball of steel wool into the jar and make sure it is well submerged to stop it from rusting. Put the lid on loosely to allow the formed gases to escape. **After a week, the steel wool is completely dissolved,** and the brew has a dark brown to black colour. To remove the last remnants of steel wool, you can pour it **through a coffee filter.** If you don't want to wait for a week, you can speed up the process by heating the

bowl in a bain-marie; then you will be ready in a day.

When you rub wood with this liquid, it **reacts with the tannins in the wood.** A chemical process that, as a layman in chemistry, seems a bit magical. The wood will quickly darken and, depending on the amount of tannins, sometimes turn completely black in a few minutes.

The wood species here in Belgium that contain the most tannins are **oak and chestnut and, to a slightly lesser extent, cherry.** Tannin is a core substance found mainly in the heartwood of heartwood trees and especially those with dark cores. Wood species such as maple or birch have few tannins, so ebonization leads to a brown colour. In itself, the different shades of brown from different wood species can generate a nice effect. Elm, for example, often gets a golden-brown colour when ebonized.

If you want to turn less suitable wood a really deep black anyway, you can **add tannins to the wood** before ebonizing. The easiest way is to make **a very strong black tea.** Instead of one teabag, use ten and let them steep much longer than usual. I wouldn't drink it anymore. Rub your wood with the tea, leave for a few minutes and then remove any residue with a cloth. Then, you can ebonize it. This way, you can turn almost all types of wood black. By repeating the ebonizing process, you can make the colour even darker or make the black more intense. When your piece is completely dry, rinse everything well under the tap. When it is dry again, you can apply a layer of oil if you like.

The pictures show a tablespoon made of chestnut. The upper part of the handle is sapwood, which contains far fewer tannins than the heartwood, and does not turn black. The bowl is not ebonized. The inside of the kuksa and the beech spoon had two coatings to turn black. The spatula is made of American oak, which contains less tannins than English oak.

BAKING

Yes, you can bake wood in the oven! The aim is to give the wood a brown to even completely black colour. I set the oven to 392°–428°F (200–220°C), so it's ideal to combine with pizza. It is important that the wood is completely dry. The oven accelerates drying, so if the wood still contains a lot of moisture, your workpiece may crack. 'Dry' means that the moisture content of the wood is in balance with its environment. In the oven, the wood can still lose extra moisture (which it will absorb later). Usually, for spoons and other carvings, this is no problem, but for shrink pots, there is a chance that the wood will shrink just a little extra. If it can't – because the bottom of the

pot doesn't shrink along with it – the pot will crack in the oven. But he who dares wins.

Baking and discolouration is difficult to predict. It depends on the type of wood, the shape, the oven and the humidity of the wood. Sometimes it is fast, sometimes it can take dozens of minutes.

So don't go too far and occasionally look through the window of your oven. It doesn't matter if your piece has already been oiled or not, but if you do it after oiling, you speed up polymerization.

Fingernail decoration and stabbing

Fingernail decoration is a specific form of 'chip carving' **using a round gouge to make cuts in wood that somewhat resemble the shape of a nail.** As it is always a succession of the same two cuts, it is much **easier to learn than other forms of chip carving,** and after some practice you can quickly achieve beautiful results. You can also combine the cuts in different patterns and directions.

The gouge I use is one with deep hollowing of ⁵/₃₂in (4mm) wide. It is actually almost half a circle with a diameter of ⁵/₃₂in (4mm). Such gouges provide the best results. The width can vary depending on the desired size of the cut.

You make **the first cut** by pushing the gouge into the wood at an angle of about 75 degrees to the wood. This cut acts as a stop cut for the next. You make **the second cut** at a certain distance from the first; in this example, ¾in (2cm). You start at about a 45-degree angle and make a scooping movement while cutting to about a 25-degree angle. The gouge ends at the notch of the first cut and this is how you cut away the chip from the piece of wood.

This technique is really beautiful when you repeat the pattern, in different directions. You always make the next first cut at a fixed distance above or beyond the previous one. The next second cut begins inside the half circle of the previous first cut, and so on. You obtain a nice effect if you cut a new row in the opposite direction. Then, you can make the first cuts of the second row following the first cuts of the first row. If you repeat this in multiple rows, the first cuts result in a wavy line.

At the end of a row you simply stop, but you can also finish with a first cut, which you cut in the opposite direction that connects nicely, and results in a circle. You should make the latter at an angle of about 110 degrees, because if you use 2 x 75 degrees, there is a risk that the wood inside the circle would break loose – which you might not want.

As you master cutting the pattern, you will come up with your own combinations. It gets even more fun when you combine it with stabbing with a knife tip. This is not really chip carving, as no wood is cut away. Instead, you push the tip of your knife or other pointed tool perpendicularly into the wood, opening up the fibres. With most knives, this creates a small opening shaped like a sharp-angled triangle. Using this, you can apply cross or star patterns or you can combine it with the round gouge which will make unexpected shapes emerge. Let your creativity go wild. It is a nice start, from which you can continue with other gouges or more difficult forms of chip carving.

09

SWIFTLY SMART SHARPENING

Theory, practice and lots of practising

Grinding or sharpening is complex, often difficult at first, but necessary – and sometimes very frustrating. When trying to find information online, sometimes you can't see the wood for the trees. Many people have convincing reasons why their approach works best and buying sharpening materials online can cause a lot of stress due to the overwhelming choice. Knives and Tools, a large online shop for knives and sharpening materials, returns 4,910 hits alone for the term 'sharpen'. **Let me help you navigate the immense offerings in the world of sharpening.**

At one time, I almost hated sharpening, and maybe that's precisely why I've become good and, more importantly, fast at it. Like cleaning up after carving, many people like sharpening less than carving itself, but it has to be done. Unless you buy new tools every time, or rely on someone else to sharpen them. **After lots of practice, experimenting and teaching others about sharpening, making and keeping tools sharp has eventually become straightforward and even soothing to me.** This knowledge and skill is also very important for restoring old tools and forging new ones, which is exactly where I get my satisfaction. **I would like to summarize the path I have taken here as basic theory and its practical translation, to keep your axe and knives razor-sharp.**

WHY SHARPENING?

What we all know, or can figure out, is that a sharp knife cuts into wood easier than a blunt one. By easier I refer to different things, though. **For one thing, you need to use less power with a sharp knife** than with a blunt knife to cut the same amount of wood. This is also why people often say that a sharp knife is safer than a blunt knife. The cutting action is more under control and by using less power you don't slide out too far. However, I personally notice that I always use the same amount of power, and a sharp knife can also potentially cause a bigger wound. So, I mostly rely on the safety tips to cut safely and always cut with a lot of power at a level that is still comfortable. **On the other hand, a sharp knife allows you to cut more wood, making the job faster.** Moreover, with a sharp knife **the wood also gets a much smoother surface,** which is difficult or sometimes not even feasible with a blunt knife.

In short, working with sharp tools is better both for yourself and for the end result of your workpiece. Moreover, **regular maintenance of your tools makes them last longer.** If you wait too long to do so, you have to take off a lot more material, which causes the tool to wear out faster. So why don't they make blades that are so hard and sharp that they never need sharpening? The very simple reason is that the material to make such knives does not exist. And what comes close is not affordable, so sharpen!

WHAT IS SHARPENING?

Sharpening is removing **metal** with an **abrasive or sharp material** from a **cutting tool in** order to obtain a **sufficiently sharp edge** on **the cutting edge – where two bevels** meet at a predetermined angle.

That is an initial, simple definition of grinding or sharpening. **However, to understand how, when, how much and what to use to sharpen, we are going to take a closer look at each part of this definition.** Getting good at sharpening takes a lot of practice. But first, you need to have a good basic understanding of the various elements that are important for successful sharpening. A blunt knife has a less sharp edge because particles of the blade have broken off in use, but an edge can also be slightly bent (or rolled) and therefore perform less well.

METAL?

Almost **all tools produced today are made of steel.** Tool steel is iron to which carbon has been added at a rate of 0.2–2%. More than 2% carbon results in cast iron, which is strong but more brittle than steel and not suitable for tools. Less than 0.2% carbon makes steel more flexible, but it cannot be hardened properly to be strong enough for cutting tools.

Hardening is a heat treatment after forging or forming a tool in which the steel is heated to a certain temperature (around 1472–1562°F/ 800–850°C for most steels) and then cooled very quickly, usually in an oil bath. This process makes the steel more wear-resistant and harder, but also more brittle. Therefore, the steel is tempered afterwards, or reheated to a lower temperature (between 356–482°F/180–250 °C, depending on the steel grade) and slowly cooled again. This makes the steel slightly less brittle and tougher. There are many steels with very different properties. Roughly speaking, we can divide them into **carbon steels and stainless steels.** Stainless steels are more resistant to rusting (100% stainless does not exist!) because other substances, such as chromium and nickel, are added to the carbon steel. There are also **special steels,** such as VG10 steel, which are extremely strong and stainless. These types are more difficult to make and therefore more expensive. The type of steel combined with the heat treatment determines its hardness. This is expressed in an **HRC value** (Rockwell C scale). That value is important for both buying the right tool and sharpening. A knife with an HRC of 54–58 is good to sharpen and strong enough, while an axe with a low HRC will be less resistant to, for example, chopping dry oak. Knives over 62 HRC, while staying sharp much longer because they are harder, are also harder to sharpen. I have tried sharpening steel of HRC 68 by hand before, but failed despite all my efforts. Stainless steel tends to be harder than carbon steel and therefore slightly harder to sharpen, but with today's sharpening methods, this distinction is of less importance nowadays than it used to be and, in my opinion, there are only advantages with stainless steel.

WHAT IS SHARP?

A second part of the definition that we take a closer look at is what we mean by sharp (or blunt). Or rather, when is an edge sharp enough? **Besides the edge itself, the sharpness of an edge is determined by the inclusive angle of the bevels.** To explain this difference, the drawing shows a cross-section of a scalpel and a wood carving knife. The inclusive or inside angle formed by both bevels is usually around 25 degrees in the case of wood carving knives, which is more than twice that of a standard scalpel. This means that if we sharpen both blades equally, the scalpel, due to the smaller angle, will be sharper and cut better.

Choosing this angle is about finding the optimal balance between sharpness and strength. If you wanted to cut into wood with a scalpel, it would break with very little force. Moreover, the wear and tear of a thin edge is higher than a blunter edge. Therefore, a heavy cleaver axe usually has a more obtuse angle of 45 or 50 degrees, because it does not need to cut but to split wood. So, this angle is important when sharpening, as you will also see below. We prefer to keep this angle; you can determine that with an angle gauge.

Scalpel

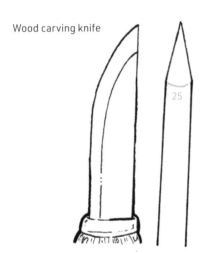

Wood carving knife

fingernail or cut through the skin of a tomato with ease. Whatever testing method you want to use, it takes experience and practice to find a good one. **Most importantly, have a method!** I always use the one for shaving hair. It is sometimes an odd sight when I have spots on my arms without hair, but this method allows me to really feel the different degrees of sharpness. It ranges from cutting no hair to a few hairs, or from a tingling sensation to numb smoothing.

Cutting paper can also give an indication, but sometimes the knife does not cut through the paper and then you know it is blunt, but not how blunt. In addition, the thickness of the paper also makes a difference. If you think your knife is sharp, try cutting through newsprint or kitchen paper in a curved shape. That requires even more sharpness than a straight cut through paper. The fingernail method gives only two possible results: the knife bites the nail, or it doesn't. To do this, put the edge of your knife on your fingernail at an angle of about 45 degrees. A sharp knife bites into your nail, a blunt knife slides over it.

There are several ways to assess the sharpness of a blade. **An estimate of sharpness or bluntness is the single most important thing you need to know or learn when it comes to sharpening.** This will not only tell you which sharpening material to start with but will also give you an indication at each intermediate step whether you are doing fine and also allows you to properly assess the end result.

Let's start with a sharp knife. For carving, this means that the knife can cut through paper easily, shave hair from your arms, 'bite' your

To give my arm hair the time to grow back, and to get an even better understanding of how sharp the tools are, **I also feel the blade with my thumb.** It is important to do this at right angles to the edge and carefully, not along the edge, because that will cause blood on your knife very quickly. This is not an easy method and takes some practice.

I also try to look very closely at **the edge of my tools.** On a really blunt knife, when you look at the top of the edge, you can see shiny pieces that reflect light. This means the edge is wider there, and wide enough to reflect the light, and therefore blunter. To look at it **more closely** for an accurate assessment, **I have a magnifying glass and a small loupe.** With a little magnification, you suddenly see so much more.

An edge – the tip of the angle formed by the two bevels – is at its sharpest theoretically only one molecule wide. Reality is different, but with a razor-sharp edge, we are talking about so many thousandths of a millimetre.

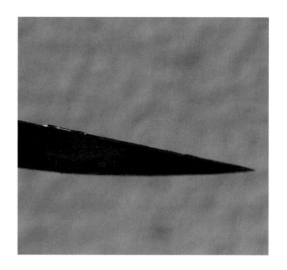

Now that we understand 'sharp', the question arises: **what is 'sharp enough'?** To me, that is when my axe and knives smoothly shave my hair without leaving me with red skin. A more logical answer would perhaps be to just test that on wood. As you probably know by now, wood is very diverse due to things like moisture, species and annual rings. My hair, fortunately, is much more consistent.

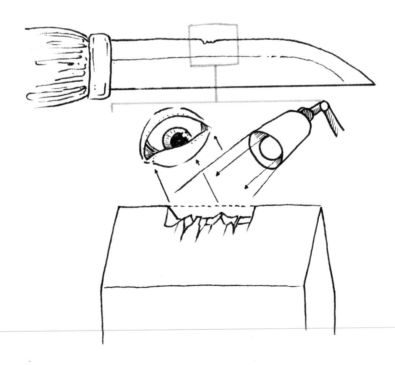

TYPES OF BEVELS

Before I can say anything about sharpening, you need to ask yourself WHAT exactly you are going to sharpen. Or rather, **what part of your knife or axe do you actually need to sharpen?** Understanding the shape of the bevels of your tool (or in other words, the shape of the two surfaces that make up the edge) is a crucial step that determines how to proceed. Not all knives and axes have the same kind of bevels. If you take a closer look at all your kitchen knives and cutting tools, you will see some differences. **We can divide these into six basic bevels,** i.e.

symmetrical bevels. There are also several types of asymmetrical bevels, as in spoon knives and the gouges I use for a shrink pot or kuksa, but your scissors at home are also asymmetrical.

The edge of each of these blades is the tip at the bottom, which we actually use to cut. The bevels are the two sides or surfaces that come together in the edge. So when we talk about sharpening, it is actually about sharpening these surfaces. **The goal is to get the edge or point between these two surfaces as thin as possible.** The photo shows an example of each kind in the same order.

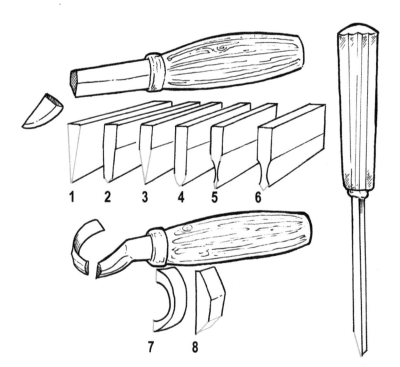

1 2 3 4 5 6

7 8

Convex

The difference between the different bevels is indicated by the green lines. When you sharpen the side surfaces, these lines indicate the contact area between the blade and grinding material. The bigger the contact area, as in the case of **the flat grind (1),** the more steel needs to be ground away to eventually have an effect only at the cutting edge. In short: the bigger, the more work. On the other hand, with the **double grind (2)** of the kitchen knife, there is less work, but the big disadvantage is that you no longer feel the angle at which you have to sharpen. So, when you put those little, short bevels on your sharpening stone, you can't feel if the bevel is flat on it. To sharpen chef's knives properly, there are all kinds of tricks or systems you can buy to ensure you can always sharpen the same angle and thus the full bevel.

With the **Scandinavian grind** of your carving knife **(3),** you do feel it, and that makes a big difference when sharpening manually. This grind actually combines the advantages of 1 and 2.

The side surfaces are large enough for manual sharpening, but not so large that it requires a lot of work.

As sharpening a flat grind is not only a lot of work, but also because there would soon not be much left of your knife, it is typically transformed to a double grind at the first sharpening. Although the angle becomes slightly larger, because the inclusive angle of the cutting edge is still small, the knife continues to cut adequately.

The convex grind (4) used to be typical for axes. It was assumed that a convex grind is stronger because there is more steel behind the edge to support it. This is sometimes true, but sometimes it is quite the opposite. As you can see in the drawing, it depends entirely on the shape of the convex grind. If you compare the black Scandinavian grind with the red convex grind, you can see that they have the same angle. However, because there is less steel in the convex grind, it is therefore less strong. The green convex grind may be wider than the red, but this also makes the angle more obtuse and the edge itself less sharp. Convex bevels are harder to sharpen with flat grinding materials, because you have to sharpen the full convexity of the side surfaces. If you only sharpen the few millimetres below the edge, you will obtain a blunt angle.

Hollow grinds are typical either on very cheap knives **(6) or**, on the contrary, on more expensive knives **(5 and 7).** The big difference is that **(6)** actually resembles the double grind **(2)**, where the first bevel is concave instead of flat. With **(5),** you can see the similarity to the Scandinavian shape, where actually the middle of the bevel is concave. This ensures that when sharpening, you have two different contact areas that are far enough apart for manual grinding, but with the great advantage that you need to grind away less material overall because the centre of the bevel is concave. At **(6),** we only have one small contact area as with the double grind.

All these bevels must be sharpened entirely, as if you were to sharpen only the cutting edge itself, you would make the angle of the knife more obtuse, which is obviously not good. On the drawing, you can see an example of what can happen if you maintain a blunter angle on a Scandinavian grind and thus sharpen only the cutting edge and not the bevels. The result depends on how consistent you are. Either you make a second bevel with a flat grind, or you round off the angle and get a convex edge. In either case, the edge will be blunter.

STAGES OF SHARPENING

Besides knowing the types of bevels and the angles you should keep, it is necessary to **know whether to start coarse or fine and what exactly it takes to get the edge sharp.** It is important here to what extent you are able to assess the sharpness yourself and can determine it correctly. The most common mistake in sharpening is to start too fine. Grinding is taking steel off the bevels with abrasive material. With coarse material, you can quickly get rid of blunt parts or gaps in your edge, but you will be left with coarse scratches. Next, you refine these scratches with increasingly finer grinding materials. Do you see the analogy with sanding wood? (See the previous chapter.) The difference between sanding wood and steel is

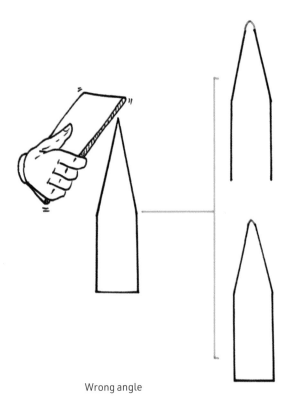

Wrong angle

that you are dealing with much finer grinding materials: from 800 grit for blunt knives to as much as 8,000 or even higher if you want to use the steel as a mirror.

The steps below are quite theoretical but will become completely clear later when grinding.

Step 1: estimate the bluntness of your knife.
Always start with shaving or paper cutting. Your knife becomes blunt gradually. If it is at the stage of just cutting off a few hairs, I would start with 1,000 grit (the number refers to the number of sharpening grains in a given area).

Hence, the smaller and finer the sharpening grains, the more of them can go in a square centimetre, and the higher the number. Note: there are different international standards that determine these numbers. 1,000 grit with one brand or type of grinding stone often means exactly the same as 1,000 grit with another stone, but not always.

The drawing shows the side view of a dull knife with missing parts, making the edge too thick to cut properly. The aim of sharpening is to use a coarse grit to grind away the edge above these gaps (i.e. up to the green line) in a small amount of time. After step 1, you are now left with an edge with coarse scratches that is not yet really sharp.

In **step 2,** you need to resharpen the edge with a finer grit, such as 2,500, to reduce the scratches. Now, the blade is already starting to cut some hair, but it wouldn't be pleasant to do a real shave yet.

In **steps 3 and 4,** repeat the operation with 4,000 grit, or even finer if you like. If everything has gone well, you can now shave reasonably well. **If you were to start using very fine grinding**

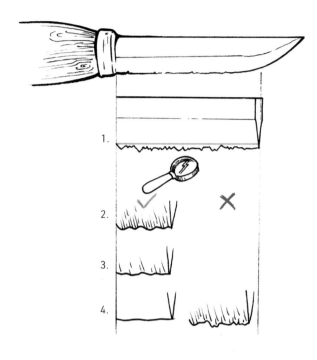

material because your sharpening method is not quite okay yet, you will get what's on the right: the highest parts of the edge are finely sharpened, but the fine grinding material works so slowly and superficially that the deeper nicks – thus, the blunt parts – are not sharpened at all. The reverse can also happen: if your knife is actually still sharp but you start sharpening using 1,000 grit, eventually your knife will be sharp again, but in the meantime you have used more time and removed more steel than necessary.

As the bevels of our knives and axes are symmetrical, it is important to more or less keep track of how many sharpening movements (turning, up and down, back and forth) you make, to ensure that you sharpen both sides equally. It doesn't have to be absolutely perfect, but if you were to constantly grind one side more than the other, you get asymmetrical bevels, which can work differently in the wood. To keep track of it in practice, you can count or sing a song while grinding, whatever works for you.

Stropping

A quick recap before we continue. You have to sharpen both bevels from coarse to fine. The coarseness with which you start depends on the bluntness of your tool. You will be able to assess that perfectly later with your sharpening system. When you sharpen a bevel, something strange happens at the cutting edge. **While sharpening, you are rubbing off steel fibres, but at the cutting edge they just don't break off. All these fibres together are called the burr.** In the drawing, the red burr is larger than in reality, but if you grind coarsely, you can even feel the burr with your fingernail. On the other side of the cut, if you try to scratch the cutting surface towards the cut with your fingernail, your nail will get stuck on the burr.

The burr is what you want to remove eventually. At each step from coarse to fine, you therefore start grinding one side first, then the other, and finally you alternate both sides several times. In a way, it works like breaking a metal paperclip. By bending it back and forth, it eventually breaks. Although there is still a burr left after fine grinding, even after alternating bevels, you can't feel it because it is very fine. **The problem is that if you are going to use this knife to cut into wood, the burr will not break off nicely and does not leave a neat sharp edge.** On the contrary, the burr will break off roughly and at the same time take a piece of the edge with it, making it blunt again faster.

To remove that last invisible burr, we are going to strop the knife. Like the barber, you do this on a piece of leather, often glued to a board. The movement you make is identical to sharpening, but the slight pliability of the leather will cause the burr to get stuck in the leather. Remember, while stropping, don't move the edge forward, otherwise you will cut the leather. I will go into more detail later when actually sharpening.

Burr

If you want to get your knife or tool extra sharp, you can rub the leather with **stropping compound.** This is a kind of chalk or paste with added abrasive particles that usually have a grain between 6,000 and 10,000. While stropping, you will thus remove the burr and, at the same time, also grind or polish your edge very finely. Now you can really smoothen your blade. The different colours of the sharpening compounds usually refer to the sharpening particles it contains.

GRINDING MATERIALS

Before you start sharpening or buy materials, it is necessary to understand what kinds of grinding materials exist and learn about their advantages and disadvantages.

01

WATER STONES

Best-known are **water stones.** These are mostly synthetic porous stones, although **natural stones are** still mined, such as our special **Belgian coticule** from the Ardennes. The latter are slightly harder and grind a bit slower, but as a result, they wear down slower. Since they are natural stones, the grain is not always consistent, which is a disadvantage with the finer grains.

Water stones get their name from the fact that you have to immerse them in water beforehand, so they are saturated before you start grinding. **The water on the stone's surface ensures that metal particles and worn grains are removed from the stone during the grinding process.** As a result, a new layer of sharp grains will be there for the next sharpening movement. Water stones are usually fairly large because they wear out quickly, though affordable. However, they are heavy to carry in your backpack and, moreover, they are fragile. **These stones are perfect for use in your workshop.**

Another disadvantage is that they can wear unevenly, i.e. grooves and hollows can be caused by continuously grinding in the same place. You can avoid this by using the entire stone, or by using another stone to flatten your used water stones again.

The biggest drawback to me, however, is the water. In the forest, I don't always have water and at home it quickly becomes a mess in my workshop – but maybe that's more down to me. Similar to water stones are **oilstones;** they use oil for the same reason water stones need water. However, they are used less and less. They have the same advantages and disadvantages as water stones, although they are slightly less porous and therefore stronger. That's also the reason why they use oil instead of water. And with oil, I make an even bigger mess.

02

SANDPAPER

Sandpaper, of course, is an option, as well. **That's the cheapest grinding method** and thanks to the internet, you don't have to go on a true treasure hunt to find sheets of 6,000 grit or even more these days. You need to stick or attach them to a flat surface, such as a board. They wear out quickly so you need to replace them sooner than other abrasives. Nevertheless, they are by far the cheapest solution, and if you are a bit handy, you can make your own boards to switch sheets quickly without having to stick them. The biggest disadvantage of sandpaper is that **you cannot grind with the edge forward** because it will cut the paper. This makes grinding slower, but you may enjoy this more than I do. When grinding a convex bevel, sandpaper is the easiest solution. Use a board to which a mousepad is glued with a sheet of sandpaper on it. If you apply the right pressure, the sandpaper will be pressed into the mousepad, making contact with the convex shape of the knife and its bevels everywhere, thus sharpening it evenly along its entire length.

CERAMIC GRINDING STONES

Due to the name, you might think that **ceramic grinding stones** have something to do with clay, yet this is usually not the case. They consist of aluminium oxide or silicon carbide in powder form. This synthetic powder is manufactured in a laboratory to obtain the desired grain size. Together with a binder, which is sometimes clay, the powder is baked into a ceramic grinding stone.

They are extremely hard and hardly wear out. They are usually sold as thin stones, implying that you should not drop them. The biggest advantage is that **no water or oil is** needed. Washing the stones once in a while to remove steel residue is enough. A disadvantage is that a different system is used to indicate grain size, and thus they do not have the same numbers as water stones or sandpaper. The typical indication is 'fine' or 'extra fine', sometimes also with the size of the grain in microns. Roughly 18 microns corresponds to 1,000 grit for sandpaper, 8 microns to 2,500 and 5 microns to 5,000. I estimate that 'fine' usually means about 800 grit, and 'extra fine' is around 2,000 grit. By themselves, the exact numbers don't matter that much.

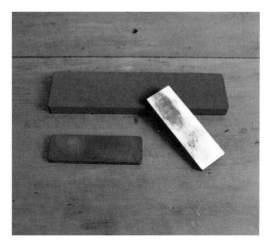

DIAMOND GRINDING STONES

These are thin stones or sometimes more like files, with a thin metal layer containing diamond grains. Since diamond is the hardest natural material, these stones hardly wear out. However, the diamond grains do not come from naturally formed diamonds but are made in a laboratory. The hardness is the same. So maybe a little less romantic, but they are fantastic stones. The small ones are very affordable. Large stones are also available but will cost as much as the average Japanese water stones. Like the ceramic stones, they do not need water, nor do they follow the grain system of sandpaper. **When new, they can feel very aggressive at the first sharpenings,** but soon get to their particular grit and optimum performance.

192

You can probably already guess my favourites. Over the years, I have collected and tried a lot of sharpening materials. What is described here is a brief summary of my journey in sharpening materials – which, by the way, cost me some

money. **For now, my journey has ended with a diamond sharpening stone for slightly coarser work and a two-sided ceramic stone for fine grinding.** Together with my stropping compound and homemade strop, this set costs only about £40. I use it to sharpen both my knife and axe. The fact that I don't know the exact grit sizes makes little difference in the end. My system with three successive grit sizes works and meanwhile, I can also link each step well with shaving my arms.

GRINDING MOVEMENTS

My grandfather swore that you should never move the grinding stone against the cutting edge of your tools, just as you should not do when stropping or sharpening with sandpaper. Others are firmly convinced that it is just the other way around. In my opinion, they are both right and wrong. **It doesn't matter! With the edge or against it, from left to right, top to bottom, turning in circles....** Grinding is taking steel off a bevel and it works well in any direction. Furthermore, **it's faster if you sharpen in all directions.** If you just push the knife forward over a stone, you have to lift the knife at the end of the stone and bring it back to the starting position every time. In doing so, you risk rounding the edge if you already start turning over the knife while it is still in contact with the stone. In the same amount of time, I have moved back and forth maybe five times. An additional advantage of sharpening in all directions is that you can also make shorter movements, thus sharpen every part of your bevels with more control. Only when grinding by machine do I take the wheel's turning direction into account. Again, it makes no difference for the grinding itself, but grinding against the direction of the edge causes the water to splash further making, again, a mess.

Grinding is watching and assessing. A golden tip is to **colour the surfaces to be sharpened with a marker,** which allows you to see where steel is removed. The most annoying thing that can happen in grinding is to grind at an incorrect angle, i.e. blunting it. It's a lot of work to fix it, much more than it took to do it wrong.

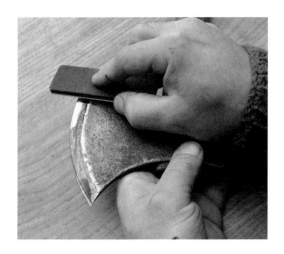

One of the most frequently asked questions during workshops is: **'How long should you sharpen at each step?'** Since that depends on the sharpness of your tool, sharpening material, hardness of your tool, speed and the pressure with which you sharpen, there is no appropriate answer here. To get you started, I would suggest that you start sharpening a sharp knife with 1,000 grit; and you count how many moves you need to get a clearly perceptible burr. That's a good indication of how many moves are needed in the next steps. For me, that's about ten moves back and forth, turning, per intermediate step. In each step, I take one side six times, then six times the other, and then alternate each four more times.

SHARPENING AXE, KNIFE AND SPOON KNIFE

The description below has grown from my experience, which means it is not the only or best way. **My sharpening system is small and portable, relatively cheap, works fast and is easy for me, but maybe not for you.** For every tool, I developed a method that works fine without clamping anything, hence I don't have to think about it. Sharpening with small stones requires that I hold both the knife and the stone in my hands simultaneously. Hence, I cannot put the sharpening stone on a table which would allow me to use both hands to hold the knife. My loose way is faster, although at first it is difficult to keep a consistent angle. That's why I also demonstrate it with a large stone further on in the book.

01

AXE

I hold my axe like you would hold a spoon during the chest grip. This way, I seek support from my body. An additional advantage is that you are looking down on top of the blade and see when the stone is lying nicely on the bevel. **You move the stone back and forth along the edge while turning in circles.** If the axe has a flat or concave grind, you can feel whether the stone is flat on the bevel. If it has a convex grind, colouring the bevel is really important to see which part you are sharpening. In that case, I start at the edge so I can see the colour disappear. If you start on the other side of the bevel, the marker is almost completely gone by the time you get to the edge itself and you cannot check whether or not you are sharpening at too much of a slant. In terms of safety, you need to make sure your fingertips don't go past the front of the sharpening stone so they can't touch the cutting edge of the axe. To make that easier, there are sharpening pucks for axes. They resemble a hockey puck, but thicker, so you have more grip and less risk of hitting the cutting edge while sharpening. **While stropping the axe,** you cannot turn it around in circles

without cutting into the leather. Consequently, you have to move away from the edge. As you can see in the photo, I make an upward movement with the strop. Your arm gets looser from your body this way, which gives you a little less control and makes looking extra important. It helps if your strop is not too big or too heavy.

02

KNIFE

Using my **loose way of sharpening knives,** I hold the knife firmly in my hand, while clamping my whole arm against my body to keep the knife as stable as possible. With my sharpening hand, I move the stone back and forth along the cutting edge, while turning in circles. I try to keep my sharpening arm against my body as much as possible, just loose enough so that I can move along the entire length of the bevel. Be careful not to slide past the tip of your blade, as you could cut yourself easily. Make sure you also sharpen the tip of your knife properly, because that bit is curved, which means you have to make a twisting motion with your stone as well.

and then, in a smooth motion, lift the handle a little to let the tip make contact so it is sharpened. You return to the beginning and repeat this. Since I prefer to sharpen quickly and move back and forth, **my solution** is **to sharpen the blade in two or three parts,** depending on the length of the blade. First, I move forward and backward quickly, while keeping contact with the straight part of the bevel continuously. Next, I slant the knife to make contact with the first part of the curve, and finally, sharpen the tip of the bevel.

Stropping the knife is done in a similar workflow, yet also only away from the edge. The first straight part of your knife is easy and quick; the curved part is a bit slower and requires more control.

As mentioned above, you have **more control with a large flat stone.** Since it is on the table, you can hold the knife with both hands and feel the cutting edge making contact with the stone even better. Start by putting the knife on your stone and tilt it to place the cutting edge flat on the stone. If you look closely, however, you will see that **the tip of your knife is not making contact,** as the edge curves upwards in the side view. A common solution is to push the knife forward

03

SPOON KNIFE

Before sharpening the spoon knife, we need to take a closer look at what the bevels look like. The photos show **two very different shapes of spoon knives,** and these also correspond to the bevels on the drawing on page 186. The spoon

knife in the photo with the yellow wooden handle is the **Mora 164 spoon knife** with bevels **(8).** On the outside, this knife has three different surfaces, while the inside is mostly flat and more convex where they bend more tightly. Since this is an asymmetrical grind, you can choose to sharpen only one of the bevels, and remove the burr on the other surface at the end after each step. On the Mora knife, the outer bevel towards the edge is significantly shorter and therefore much easier to sharpen. However, due to its very

curved shape, it is difficult to follow with a stone in your hand. If you can clamp the spoon knife while sharpening, it's a bit easier to sharpen the different parts of the curve.

When sharpening the **other spoon knife with a hollow inside and curved outside (7),** it is much easier and faster to sharpen the inside. **For this, I sawed dowels to size and wrapped them with 1,000 and 2,500-grit sandpaper, and another with a piece of leather with stropping compound.** Make sure the diameter is smaller than the roundness of your spoon knife, so you can reach every bit. Push your arms close to your body and hold your spoon knife as steady as possible. Start with the stick on the inside of your

sharpen the entire bevel in one smooth move. If you try this with the Mora knife, your hand moves all the way to the other side at the last part of the curve and you can hardly keep the bevel flat on the stone. It works fine though for Wood Tools' spoon knives with an open curve.

spoon knife at the handle and make sure it makes good contact with both contact points of the hollow bevel. Your wrist is tilted inwards to begin. Push the stick forward and meanwhile sideways towards the curve of your spoon knife, while turning the stick outwards with a wrist movement. This allows you to sharpen the entire inside in one smooth motion. Since the burr is now formed on the outside, again, after each intermediate step, I move the stick very slowly along the outside, right up against the edge.

A third way of sharpening or stropping **a spoon knife** works very well when the knife has less curvature. The spoon knife in this example is very useful for smoothing shallow eating spoons and I also strop it on the outside. The motion is the same if you wanted to sharpen a knife with a bevel on the outside, but on a stone. Hold the spoon knife underhand and put the beginning of the bevel on the strop. Push the knife forward while making a twisting motion with your wrist to

CONCLUSION

To me, this chapter was perhaps the biggest challenge of this book. When translating movements into words, even with pictures attached, I miss the interaction and the ability to show the fine nuances of the movements. If sharpening is new to you, this chapter will not be easy. **Focus on different sections, reread them, test what I write using online videos, and above all, practise and practise.** As you gain experience, you will gain different insights or other questions will come to mind. If you then revisit this chapter, the explanations will become clearer and more self-evident.

To conclude, I'd like to repeat the **main reasons why sharpening sometimes fails:**
You are not maintaining the angle because your sharpening tool is not constantly flat on your bevel. Check using the colouring method and see what happens while sharpening. If you have rounded the cut – thus, made it blunt – you can sometimes even see this with the naked eye. Then, it's time to ask for help to flatten it again.

You do everything right and still the tool isn't sharp. It means you didn't start sharpening coarsely enough at the beginning or you didn't take long enough for the intermediate steps. Feel, shave and cut paper to check whether an intermediate step made a difference.

I will end with some answers to questions that very often come up during the sharpening workshops I do. Have fun sharpening!

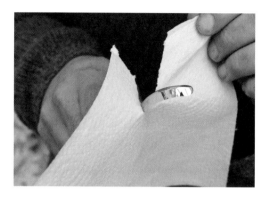

SHARPENING TIPS AND TRICKS

Which leather is best for a strop?
Untreated or unpainted, i.e. natural light brown leather works best, but is certainly not necessary. The main requirement is that the leather absorbs the compound well, which is difficult with leather that has a pattern pressed into it or has a shiny finish. In that case, it is better to use the bottom if it is not too frayed.

How do you clean a strop?
After a few strops, the leather is saturated with steel particles resulting in a smooth, hard black layer. Simply rinse under the tap and use, for example, the back of a knife to scratch off the black layer.

Why grind with a machine using water?
The water constantly cools the steel. These machines also tend to run a bit slower. With machines without water, there is a greater risk of overheating the edge and degrading the hardness of your tool. But with practice and regular cooling of the blade, it can be done.

Machines cost a lot of money and it was only after years that it became worthwhile to me because of a lot of sharpening and restoring old tools. Always learn to sharpen manually, I'd suggest; incorrect grinding with a machine immediately has a greater impact.

A Tormek grinder has only one stone with 1,000 grit. So, what about the tip to grind in several steps?

A machine is tireless. So after 1,000 grit, you switch to the leather with paste. Manually, you would need a lot of time and strength to make that big jump, but the machine does all the work for you.

What is a sharpening steel and how does it differ from a sharpening rod?

If you have one of those round sticks with a handle like chefs often use, it could be both. But there is a big difference. A sharpening steel does not sharpen and therefore does not take off steel, but by rubbing the cutting edges at the right angle, it allows you to straighten a thin edge, making the knife cut more effectively. A sharpening rod actually sharpens and takes off material. You can tell the difference between both by the material of the bar. A sharpening steel is always made of steel, while a sharpening rod is usually made of ceramic or diamond, like sharpening stones.

Can I use a kitchen sharpener for my wood carving knives?

I wouldn't do that! Such a thing has only one angle and actually works very aggressively. You quickly get a burr, which 'bites' well in soft material like fruit or vegetables, but (as described above) the blade becomes blunt again faster when the burr starts to wear off.

Which grinding paste is best to buy?

I have used different types and have not noticed any major differences. Of course, it also depends on how far you want to go in sharpening or polishing your tools. Grit 6,000 is sufficient for me, but some pastes are even finer. Fällkniven's green blocks are small and last a long time. Don't be tempted to buy big blocks. I really grind a lot and have blocks I won't run out of in my lifetime.

How hard should I push while grinding?

The harder you can push, the faster you can sharpen. But more force often also means less control and a greater risk of not being able to maintain the right angle. When sharpening, force is always secondary to precision.

WOOD CARVING IS GOOD FOR US

The core of craftsmanship is freedom

I HOPE THAT IN THIS BOOK I WAS ABLE TO SHARE MY JOY, PASSION AND EXPERIENCE IN GREEN WOOD WORKING WITH YOU. Hopefully, it has encouraged you to try it yourself or make (more) time for it.

Every day I work with fresh wood, but I am not a lone craftsman in my workshop. My passion concerns trees, wood, tools and, perhaps most of all, people. There are many special things about my work, but what touches me again and again are the pleasant encounters with cheerful people. That gives me energy and the desire to keep doing it and do it even better. Working with green wood using hand tools does something to us. I believe in it and I am proud of what I do for many different reasons, and that is what this final chapter is about. Wood carving is good for you and me, for us and for our planet!

I'VE NEVER DONE IT BEFORE...

... so I'm sure I can do it. This statement, often attributed to Pippi Longstocking (although she never said it herself in the series or books) brims with self-confidence. Or maybe it's more like an attitude or positive way of undertaking something new in our lives. Unfortunately, reality rarely feels so easy and few go through life as surely as Pippi. Picasso once said: 'Every child is an artist, the problem is to remain an artist growing up.' We often experience barriers when starting something new. Our adult lives are sometimes so much more complicated than the carefree lives of Pippi and her friends. Children are still allowed to play and unleash their creativity. As adults, we often have to perform without failure. However, **the difference between failure and success lies precisely in trying.** Learning to love imperfection in something made with love lowers the threshold for starting something. Creating something new and growing means precisely being allowed to make mistakes in order to learn from them.

There are always reasons why we should not start a new hobby, but sometimes you just have to do it. Just start. Throughout my life, I have often convinced myself that **starting something is half the way there.** Writing this book was no different. Unfortunately, we don't always know in advance the very reasons why we should start something – that's when we need some confidence. Getting good at wood carving is a journey that never ends but has to start somewhere.

A new hobby, new materials, new tools; even green wood working can seem challenging for many people at first. And it gets even tougher when we add the wise saying that you need '10,000 hours of practice to get something right'. Of course, a certain level of commitment is needed, and practice makes an art and craft. **But working in green wood using hand tools is incredibly accessible at several levels:**

THE WOOD

A branch or a piece of log, that's all it takes to get started. Many people have wood in the garden and others can easily obtain a piece of wood in other ways. It is free, local, transportable and – if you have the necessary knowledge about the drying process – workable for a long time. **Wood grows on trees and fortunately they grow almost everywhere.** There is no distinction between better or more exclusive wood species. Perhaps that one tree with fungus from your garden is precisely why it is so special and unique.

THE TOOLS

Using just a knife, a piece of wood and their own hands, it is incredible what some people can create. If you would rather work on larger pieces, then an axe and saw come into play. But even then, **in terms of cost and tool availability,** it is **extremely accessible to almost everyone.** People who know me often laugh when I repeat how few tools you actually need. They know that my workshop is full of knives, axes, gouges, adzes, saws, drawknives and much more. Though, when I travel, everything I need fits into a small backpack. And especially in those relaxed moments, I often create the most beautiful things.

AGE OR GENDER

I teach wood carving to children as young as six, carving simple basic pieces, such as a butterknife or magic wand. Initially, parents are often worried about giving a sharp knife to their children. Of course, it is important to properly teach adapted grips and provide safety instructions in accordance with their age and understanding. Also, each child is different. After a year of teaching at the Steiner School, it was incredible to see what the 11-year-old children could do after a weekly hour of wood carving. On the other hand, I also know a 91-year-old man who still makes all kinds of small utensils and handles for tools in green wood almost every day. **Muscle power is secondary to technique, skill, creativity and enthusiasm.**

Although it occurs less frequently, I still sometimes hear the prejudice that wood working is mainly something for men. During my first courses, the participants consisted mainly of men. In recent years, this has evolved into an equal distribution between men and women. **At the Spoon Club, too, the division is nice and, above all, cosy.**

THE WORKSHOP

For smaller works, you need almost no space: a chair to sit and maybe a small chopping block to go with it. It can be done on a bench in the park or on a stump in the woods, in the smallest flat or just somewhere on the road. Even the fully equipped workshop of an artisan chair maker is

smaller and cheaper than that of the average cabinetmaker who uses machines. My workshop is adjacent to our living room and although I sometimes scatter scraps throughout the rest of our house, those are cleaned up quickly. **Sometimes I also just carve at the kitchen table;** then I can work and be part of the family at the same time. Children are allowed (even more so in the past than now, I think) to paint, craft, draw, make slime and much more at home at the kitchen table. So why aren't we allowed to do some carving (and clean up nicely afterwards, of course)?

THE FINAL PRODUCT

Green wood working is incredibly versatile and broad. There is an almost unlimited number of possibilities of what can be made from a fresh branch or trunk. **Something for everyone!** Think of utensils, interior products, decorative work, jewellery and ornaments, furniture, small or large projects. There is no preset goal and you can design your home, time and money as it fits and feels right for you. To me, green wood carving is a big part of my life, present every day; for someone else it might be just that one relaxing moment on a trip to carve something at the campfire. Who knows what it can do for you!

TALENT

It is very difficult to define what talents you should have in the differentiated actions that green wood projects require. This also raises the question if something is the result of talent or experience and hours of practice. I make no judgment on this very complex relationship. My point is that while talent in some is clearly reflected by the speed in which they learn or in the products they make, **anyone can learn wood**

carving and find satisfaction and pleasure in making things. Never before during a workshop or course have I thought that someone was hopeless; often, on the contrary, people who are less skilled find even more pride and satisfaction in what they make.

Sometimes I also teach people with disabilities, both mental and physical. They often struggle with what they can or cannot do (anymore) or sometimes are allowed to do. The fun, wonder and especially the victory over fears or limitations at such moments are very touching and special!

CARVING TOGETHER

As green wood working is so broad and approachable, and also not noisy or dusty, carving in green wood is particularly suitable for **doing it together.** The Spoon Club in Bruges, Belgium has 40 participants every month. On Thursday evenings, everyone is welcome. I provide tools, a snack and a drink, and every month I bring a new fresh type of wood to discover. There is no predefined lesson content, everyone makes what they want and I help where necessary with tips and explanations. **Sounds fun and it is, but carving together is much more than that.**

Whereas most **Spoon Club** participants have already attended a basic workshop, and I provide input in terms of knowledge, technique and creativity, the Spoon Club is mainly a time for exchange. **Carving together makes you learn from each other and get inspired by other designs or ways of working.** It shows how people evolve and can gain confidence in their own growth. Through discussions and difficulties, new ideas, applications or solutions emerge. Participants sometimes also bring their own special wood to share or new tools that you can try out before purchasing something yourself. If getting to Bruges is feasible for you, be sure to come and have a taste.

There is likely to be a club not far from wherever in the world you live. **Or why not start your own wood carving club?** You don't have to be a specialist to bring people together. Working in pairs is often more fun than working alone and a whole group brings so much more than you would ever experience or learn on your own.

Besides the content, sharing a passion or hobby together is fun. For some, the social aspect is the most important. It gives people a scheduled moment in their agendas to be creative for themselves and be able to share it with others. Sometimes the Spoon Club is as quiet as a mouse and on other evenings people are roaring with laughter. Some stay in the background, others not at all. Some are friends, while others only just know each other by name. **The beauty is that the common passion makes everyone equal and connects us, no matter how different we are.**

Besides the 'club feeling', **wood carving** is **sometimes the ideal means to achieve other social goals.** I regularly work with schools to accommodate pupils in a Time-Out project. The pupils have a creative activity that addresses skills other than traditional school skills, and in between there is room for conversation, reflection and connection. I also run a project every autumn to support men's mental health through wood carving. Here, weekly carving is the way to reactivate and reconnect a group of men from different backgrounds and issues with each other and the outside world.

In the Spoon Forest, groups of disabled people from institutions come to help with all kinds of tasks, and meanwhile there is space for workshops in bushcraft or wood carving. **Nature brings peace to those who need it.**

Even broader are the **demonstrations and storytelling events** I provide on request. This way, I can easily reach a larger group of people with one activity.

If you are excited about the idea of carving with others, there is already a Spoonfest **in Flanders, in Belgium** (www.lepelfeest.be). I organize this festival together with Mr Teelepel. A special weekend, with like-minded souls, lots of wood and conviviality, sharp tools and crispy waffles. Everyone is welcome! If you don't live in Belgium, there are also Spoon Festivals in the UK and the

Netherlands – and annual weekends and gatherings in other countries too. It's still a small world, but it grows a little more every day, and it's nice to be part of it.

VIRTUOUS CRAFTSMANSHIP

It is fantastic to see what a day of working with your hands can do to a person. Almost always during workshops, I notice that people are in a kind of flow after working for several hours and are totally focused on their work, their hands and their creation. Some describe it as very relaxing; for others it is almost therapeutic. Many students describe the peace as 'very pleasant' or 'rare'; others stress the group experience and the cosy atmosphere. Some 'modern' wood workers enjoy the silence or the absence of machines. Others are proud – they did not think they could create something so basic, beautiful and functional in just a few hours.

I see people feeling and smelling the wood, others want to know all about the trees and the origin of the wood. People with a technical background often want to know more about traditional tools and others are already looking forward to finishing, painting or decorating their pieces. Children and young people often seem less aware of the process; for them, it often feels more natural and self-evident to play and create with your hands.

In all the years I have been teaching green wood working, I have noticed that **it always does something to people, no matter how different they are.** A simple explanation is that working with your hands is so fundamentally human and we need it in our lives. Unfortunately, manual work is all too often rated lower than mind work, and children are given far less opportunity or encouragement to use their hands. This not only results in less developed physical skills, but also in more limited development of their spatial insight and feeling

for design. **So, it is not merely the handwork, but the mind and heart working together with the hands to create something.**

Creativity is a journey through past and present people, materials, techniques and connection. In our current society, full of mechanization and digitalization, creativity is sometimes hard to find, although that shouldn't really be a contradiction. Wood carving is taking away wood; what you want to make is already in the wood. You can't add anything more to it or start over with the same piece of wood as you would with clay if your work collapses. That creates both a barrier and a challenge when working in wood. **Wood carving is both creation and discovery.**

Being able to be creative means freedom. Free to experiment or play. Free at every step of the process to carve your own knowledge and skill, as well as your own story, into the wood. For many people, the freedom we experience while creating is unique and in great contrast to the expectations and obligations of our daily lives. This freedom provides great satisfaction when finishing something and is very different from the short-term satisfaction we experience with anything involving zapping and swiping. Satisfaction and pride in yourself, no matter how small, can sometimes be incredibly important to someone. Sometimes, these small steps are instrumental in realizing that you can do something on your own, while the extension to other aspects of life becomes more achievable.

This freedom and the associated satisfaction is therefore a fundamental difference from machine-based mass production. In green wood processing as a craft, the entire process from the fresh wood to the product is a succession of choices and possibilities. This not only makes the end result unique, but, especially, the process itself is special. **At its core is the freedom and expression of the maker – freedom as the counterpart of perfection. So it does not matter where the energy during creation comes from.**

As I mentioned, machines certainly have a place in a contemporary workshop. They make things faster or less stressful for the body. However, it is the freedom we need to preserve. When the constraints of a machine – or a teacher – begin to guide or limit your creativity, we lose what is at the heart of handwork. We see the best example of this in all the straight lines and 90-degree angles in our houses, furniture and so on. Machines simply cut straight lines the easiest and fastest. In my workshops, I therefore try to find the balance between structured teaching and the freedom of each trainee to make what she or he wants.

That crafts can be virtuous is also reflected in what is described as **'flow'**. This is a special mindset you can be in when you are very focused on creative handwork. Flow is hard to describe

and certainly not easy to explain. Anyone who has experienced it will know what I mean. For me, flow is **a combination of intense focus and creative pleasure** and can perhaps be compared to the intensity of a child's play. Sometimes children become so absorbed in their experience that the world around them no longer seems to exist. As adults, we have forgotten this and through mindfulness, yoga or meditation we try to find that feeling again of being completely focused on ourselves and our bodies. To me, flow doesn't mean shutting off the outside world completely, but that the focus on your craft creates a kind of filter where thoughts and any worries enter more slowly and sometimes less overwhelmingly.

The intention is not to shut out all thoughts, but the detachment we experience in a flow state can allow us to step back for a moment and then approach a problem with fresh eyes or new solutions. This implies the special value of craft in general and even more so of wood carving in particular because of its great accessibility.

SUSTAINABLE CRAFT

The price of a handmade spoon is many times higher than a metal spoon from an interior design shop. However, the total cost to our society is much smaller. Making something requires energy. In green wood working, you are talking mainly about muscle power and, to a limited extent, transport of the wood and tools. Imagine how much energy it takes to make a spoon out of metal and send it around the world. How much energy in mining, transporting, smelting, transporting again, manufacturing, shipping and selling is required for this! **A craft like green wood working – which works with a very local and highly sustainable raw material while requiring extremely little energy in making it – is particularly commendable, if you ask me.**

Crafts have had an old-fashioned connotation for a long time, but I am happy to see a renewed appreciation for handcrafts. Crafts provide social cohesion, strengthen the local economy and can boost tourism. In this context, **the *Handmade in Bruges* label** deserves special mention as a fine example of a support organization for local crafts and makers in Belgium. There seems to have been a gap in the training and continuation of crafts due to industrialization in the 20th century. In Flanders, there was no decent training anywhere for 100 years. I am proud to be at the cradle of what is sometimes called **'the new wood culture'.** Based on a long tradition and knowledge, on the one hand I want to look for innovative forms in the design of my products that attract both young and old, and above all, are sustainable. **With a little care and maintenance, a well-carved utensil will last a lifetime.** But even more important to me is passing on and reviving this age-old craft that brings people and wood together in a unique creative way. **I also want to help raise awareness that it really matters how the things we buy are made and what the real cost is.**

Besides my passion and love for wood, I therefore consider my daily work as a small act of resistance against mass consumption and production, but also a bit against the world of Art with a big 'A'. This is another reason **why I never sign my objects** or provide them with a 'maker's mark'. While I can be genuinely proud of what I make, it has never felt necessary or right to me.

Art and craft are linked and sometimes overlap. It is difficult to define the difference, but I think the **core of the distinction lies in the utility value of crafted objects,** which is not a prerequisite in art per se. I can sometimes really enjoy and be moved by art, by the talent and skill of its creator, or by the message a work of art can convey. However, what I have never understood **is why people pay so much more (or less) for the same or similar work of art just because of its creator.** A painting by Da Vinci is worth millions, but should his name not be on it, or it cannot be proven to be his, the same painting would be worth almost nothing. This shows that in the end it is no longer about the painting itself, the talent of the painter or the hours of training and practice it took to reach such a level.

What it shows is contained in the most concise definition of economics: the study of scarcity. An artist creates a limited number of works during his lifetime and if these are valued for whatever reason, the principle of scarcity comes into play. Da Vinci's works are worth a lot of money; first because they were valued, but eventually mainly because they are scarce. **Then some people are able to buy them and others are not.**

I don't make art, but **I hope that what I make is appreciated for what it is and even more for how**

it is made. **Nothing more and nothing less.**
I like to make basic and everyday objects that
are really used. It is **precisely in the use of** a
spoon or bag, perhaps every day, for years, **that
the quality of the product and how it is made
can really be appreciated.** Personally, I like to
surround myself with objects that are well-made
and sustainable, that are useful or beautiful. And
preferably a combination of all four. Therefore,
it is not necessary to attach my name to my work
to make its quality clear. If I were a blacksmith,
maybe I would. It is difficult to judge at first
sight how and with what steel or material
a knife is made.

A second reason why I don't sign anything is
because, to me, **the greatest pleasure and
satisfaction is in the making,** rather than in the
final product. I enjoy the search for wood among
the trees, the surprise when I split the wood,
working with hand tools and the eternal search
for originality and beautiful design. In this sense,
for me, every unmarked spoon is **an ode to the
process,** to the craft and to the tree that supplied
the wood. Once I have finished something – no
matter how proud I can be at that moment – my
interest and focus soon shift to a new piece of
wood and the **desire to create something new.**

I have never made anything I could not separate
from. That's **the third reason** why I don't sign.
Everything I make is mine for a while, but after
that, when someone buys it or gets it, it spreads
into the world. I hope the objects I make trigger
something in people or inspire them and make
them feel connected. I hope my objects are part
of beautiful stories among people and that the
wood may live on in the homes and hearts of
others. **That is a craftsman's dream.**

Thank you for reading this book!

Harald

BIBLIOGRAPHY

Many books have inspired me over the years and, in writing this book, given me knowledge and enriched my life as a craftsman. Next to green wood craft, reading is my second passion. Below is a valuable selection to help you delve further into the various themes of this book.

TREES AND FORESTS

David Suzuki & Wayne Grady, *Tree: a life story*, 2019
Jonathan Drori, *Een reis om de wereld in 80 bomen*, 2019
Guido Tack, *Bossen van Vlaanderen: een historische ecologie*, 1993
Riet Wille & An Candaele, *Toen een tak mij tikte: verhalen en gedichten over bomen*, 2021
Owen Johnson & David More, *Collins tree guide*, 2004
Patrick Jansen & Mark van Benthem, *Bosbeheer en biodiversiteit*, 2008
Colin Tudge, *The secret life of trees: how they live and why they matter* 2006
Jeroen Toirkens & Jelle Brandt Corstius, *Borealis: trees and people of the northern forest*, 2020
Valerie Trouet, *Wat bomen ons vertellen: een geschiedenis van de wereld in jaarringen*, 2020

WOOD

Richard Jones, *Cut & dried: a woodworker's guide to timber technology*, 2018
Marije Verbeeck, *1 boom, en 73 vormgevers in hout*, 2014
Bryan Nash Gill, *Woodcut*, 2012
Agentschap voor Natuur en Bos, *Cursus bosbekwaamheid: Hout – Eigenschappen en soortherkenning*, 2006
Wim Tavernier, *Hout dat spreekt: over de sterke band tussen de mens en hout*, 2021
R. Bruce Hoadley, *Understanding wood: a craftsman's guide to wood technology*, 2000

WOOD CARVING, GREEN WOODWORKING AND TOOLS

D. Cook, *The ax book: the lore and science of the woodcutter*, 1981
Ej Osborne, *Spoon carving*, 2017
Wille Sundqvist, *Swedish carving techniques*, 1990
Joshua Klein, Mortise & Tenon magazine, *Different vintages*
Joshua Vogel, *The artful wooden spoon: how to make exquisite keepsakes for the kitchen*, 2015
Samina Langholz & Andrea Brugi, *Houtbewerking: traditionele vaardigheden voor het moderne huis*, 2019
Max Bainbridge, *The urban woodsman: a modern guide to carving spoons, bowls & boards*, 2016

Jögge Sundqvist, *Slöjd in wood*, 2016
Sjors van der Meer & Job Suijker, *Lepelhout*, 2020
Charles A. Heavrin, *The axe and man*, 1988
Max Bainbridge, *Heirloom wood: a modern guide to spoons, bowls, boards and other homewares*, 2016
Nick Gibbs, Quercus (magazine), *Woodworking by hand*
Danielle Rose Byrd, *The handcarved bowl: design & create custom bowls from scratch*, 2021
Felix Immler, *Whittling in the wild*, 2019
Brett McLeod, *American axe: the tool that shaped a continent*, 2020
Paul Adamson, *Kuksa: a guide to hand carved wooden cups*, 2018
Peter Buchanan-Smith, *Axe handbook*, 2021
Sean Hellman, *Sharp*, 2021
Peter Hjortberger, *The abc of knives*, 2018

CRAFT IN GENERAL AND INSPIRING STORIES

Mihály Csíkszentmihályi, *Flow: psychologie van de optimale ervaring*, 2020
Soetsu Yanagi, *The unknown craftsman: a Japanese insight into beauty*, 2013
Canopy Press, *Force & carve – heritage crafts: the search for well-being and sustainability in the modern world*, 2018
Tom Brown Jr., *Grandfather: a Native American's lifelong search for truth and harmony with nature*, 1993
Richard Louv, *Last child in the woods: saving our children from nature-deficit disorder*, 2006
William S. Coperthwaite, *A handmade life: in search of simplicity*, 2007
Richard Sennet, *The craftsman*, 2008
George Nakashima, *The soul of a tree: a woodworker's reflections*, 1981
Monroe Robinson, *The handcrafted life of Dick Proenneke*, 2021
Drew Langsner, *Country woodcraft: then and now*, 2020
Tapis plein vzw en Handmade in Brugge, *Een toekomst voor ambachten*, 2014
Rosemary Davidson & Arzu Tahsin, *Craftfulness*, 2018

Afterword

BY LYNN DEDEYNE

I AM THE WIFE OF AN AXEMAN. Of a man who in recent years rediscovered his roots, multiplied his passion, blossomed into a green wood craftsman of fine craftsmanship and has since been carrying that out into the open, inspiring thousands. Proudly and with great admiration, I write this epilogue to a book that is the result of years of self-taught learning, self-study via dozens of books, hours of flow experiences and gathering knowledge across borders. Harald has passed on the craft as a master and has continued to challenge himself every day to grow further. His perfectionism has made this book a feat, but his self-awareness and perseverance have above all produced a lived-in result.

Writing such a book is like writing a reference work about a part of your own life, a legacy for the children and grandchildren and hopefully a timeless source of inspiration for many people. It took off with the requests from course participants to make the abundant information during a workshop day available afterwards and realizing that, in the meantime, he had gathered a lot of knowledge and experience that he wanted to share with many more people than he had reached so far. It became a dream, until it was picked up by Heidi from Lannoo publishers and by Jonathan from GMC. So, Harald wrote a book that is tailor-made for him. A theoretical, sound basis plus very detailed descriptions when tackling the projects, with a passion for beautiful and clear photos. When writing this, he had to restrain himself, otherwise it would have been a 500-page book. Meanwhile, his head is already full of ideas for a second and even third book.

Harald is a storyteller and an orator; his book is peppered with stories and other sprinkles. I, along with the other readers (Jan, An and Jonas), have tried, while going through the manuscript, to polish his storytelling personality in this book into written language. Still, I hope that between the lines, alongside all the knowledge, you can read and feel his gentleness and warmth. And that you may see and get to know the same Harald as myself, his children, his family, his friends and the thousand trainees over the past few years.

Heart for Wood (the title in Dutch) or *Green Wood Carving* is about green wood working, one of the many crafts that have been lost in Flanders. It is perplexing to see that other countries managed to keep several crafts alive over the past century and that they have survived in small, local communities, craft schools and handmade festivals. This book is a symbol of the revival in Flanders.

In my own 'studio of slöjd', I try to use various crafts such as tape weaving, wool spinning and nail binding, braiding with natural materials, weaving and knotting with fibres, pottery... to provide our own household with objects.

'Slöjd' is a Swedish teaching method and vision that emphasizes the process based on tradition, folklore and the quality of craftsmanship. After learning the basic skills, you measure yourself against a number of intrinsic goals and engage in ever-increasing complexity, experiencing great satisfaction and enjoyment. During such a flow experience, the fretting, worries, emotions and stress are momentarily gone and we become one with the environment as it seems to direct us with a magic wand. During flow, consciousness is in deep concentration and well-structured. This lifts our life to a higher level: alienation becomes involvement, boredom becomes pleasure, helplessness becomes control and mental energy empowers itself.

When crafting becomes a craft or real skill or even your job, it is hard not to fall into the traps of today's economy. I often notice that handmade items are in danger of losing their authenticity because they are commercialized and styled with lots of bells and whistles. Perhaps, like the spoon carvers themselves, all makers should switch to a new, old-fashioned form of trade: barter. I knit a Scandinavian jumper in exchange for tableware in ceramics.

I hope this book is an inspiration to you. That you may experience intense flow moments while trying out the (at first sight) complex challenges in the different projects. Or that you can be amazed by how a life can suddenly turn out differently if you follow your heart. I hope the steps Harald has taken so far are as inspiring for you as they are for me every day.

Lynn Dedeyne

First published by Uitgeverij Lannoo nv
© 2023, Lannoo Publishers, for the original edition
Original title: Hart voor hout. Vers hout ontdekken en bewerken.
www.lannoo.com

This edition published 2024 by GMC Publications Ltd,
Castle Place, 166 High Street, Lewes,
East Sussex, BN7 1XU, UK.

Text © Harald Lamon, 2024.
www.lepelhuis.be

PUBLISHER Jonathan Bailey
PRODUCTION Jim Bulley
SENIOR PROJECT EDITOR Susie Behar
EDITOR Alexis Harvey
DESIGN MANAGER Robin Shields
DESIGNER Ginny Zeal
PHOTOGRAPHY Amaurie Coudeville and Veronique De Walsche – ARTIFIX
GRAPHIC DESIGN Katrien Van de Steene for Whitespray
COLOUR ORIGINATION GMC Reprographics

Printed and bound in China

To order a book, contact:
GMC Publications Ltd
Castle Place, 166 High Street,
Lewes, East Sussex, BN7 1XU
United Kingdom
Tel: +44 (0)1273 488005

www.gmcbooks.com

FSC
www.fsc.org
MIX
Paper | Supporting
responsible forestry
FSC® C144853